William

Also available from Continuum in the Writers' Lives Series:

William Shakespeare

WILLIAM BAKER

continuum

Continuum International Publishing Group

The Tower Building   80 Maiden Lane
11 York Road   Suite 704, New York
London SE1 7NX   NY 10038

www.continuumbooks.com

British Library Cataloguing-in-Publication Data
A catalogue record for this book is available from the British Library.

ISBN: 978-1-8470-6408-0 (hardback)
   978-1-8470-6409-7 (paperback)

Library of Congress Cataloging-in-Publication Data
A catalog record of this book is available from the Library of Congress.

Typeset by Newgen Imaging Systems Pvt Ltd, Chennai, India
Printed and bound in Great Britain by MPG Books Ltd, Bodmin, Cornwall

In memory of my late mother Mabel Woolf Baker
who encouraged my love of
Shakespeare

Contents

Preface and Acknowledgements

This book is a reassessment of Shakespeare's life and work. The present study for the Continuum Writers' Lives series examines Shakespeare's output from his earliest work through his 'mature' drama and the late plays. It largely eschews speculation of a biographical, critical or textual nature and focuses instead on an account of what is known of Shakespeare and his achievements at the end of the first decade of the twenty-first century.

Shakespeare, it goes without saying, has been the subject of a tremendous amount of attention, but that focus has generally been on a particular aspect or feature. For instance, René Weis's recently published *Shakespeare Revealed* (2007) is a biographically orientated approach. It claims to put forward new and radical theories about the assumed identity of the subject of the sonnets, the Dark Lady. Clare Asquith in *Shadowplay* (2005) argues that Shakespeare's dramas contain covert codes that convey their author's Catholic beliefs. To take two other examples, Steven Greenblatt in his *Will in the World* (2004), speculates that there are connections between an entertainment presented to Queen Elizabeth on a visit to the countryside during Shakespeare's boyhood and passages in *A Midsummer Night's Dream* while Germaine Greer's *Shakespeare's Wife* (2007) speculates openly on the life of its subject.

None have comprehensively, thoroughly examined Shakespeare's total oeuvre and placed it in the perspective of what is known of Shakespeare's life and activities. This present book takes into account our current knowledge of Shakespeare's biography. It provides a consensus of textual, critical and theatrical awareness. The study reviews, where pertinent, various theories relating to Shakespeare's life and work, such as for instance, his assumed Catholic connections, and associations with the Earls of Essex and Southampton. The emphasis, though, is not on the counterfactual, but on the factual. Of course, there is bias. My preference has been for, on the one hand, the factual evidence based upon reliable documentation and, on the other hand, for the textual, for book history and what it reveals. Further, my focus is upon genre, the Comedies, the Histories, the Tragedies, the Problem Plays, the Late Plays. From these, *The Merchant of Venice*, *Twelfth Night*, *Parts 1 and 2 Henry IV, Henry V, Hamlet, Measure for Measure* and *The Tempest* will be emphasized as representative instances of their respective genres.

My debts are many and especially to those who have previously laboured in Shakespeare's vineyard. In the first instance, I'd like to thank my publisher Anna Fleming and her colleague Colleen Coalter at Continuum for providing me with the opportunity to write this book. Secondly, thanks must go to undergraduate and graduate students and colleagues in the Department of English, Northern Illinois University for encouragement and who over the years have shared my enthusiasm and love for Shakespeare. In addition, thanks must go to Professor Donald Hawes formerly of the University of Westminster, Professor Lisa Hopkins of Sheffield Hallam University, and Linda Reinert of Northern Illinois University for their judicious observations on the manuscript and to Jayne Crosby-Lindner for once again, with good humour, managing to decipher my chicken scratch. Mention must be made of former teachers who stimulated my interest in 'Shakers': the late F. R. Lewis at Hove Manor County Secondary Modern School, Hove, the late 'Rastus Randall' and Jack Smithiers at Brighton Hove and Sussex Grammar School. As an undergraduate at the University of Sussex too, in the early 1960s, I was very fortunate that my teachers, the late Professor David Daiches, the late Stephen Medcalf and Gabriel Josipovici, were ever encouraging. Thanks must also go to Lawrence Lipking and to a scholar and critic whom I never had the good fortune to meet: the late J. W. Lever, editor of *Measure for Measure* in the Arden Second Series. Above all, thanks must go to the dedicatee of this work who presented me as a schoolboy with my treasured copy of *The Tudor Edition of William Shakespeare The Complete Works*, edited by Peter Alexander and published in 1951. Of course, on another personal level, thanks are due to my wife, Rivka, who puts up with my addictions.

Abbreviations

The listing of abbreviations and references also acknowledges much indebtedness to the works, editions and contributors listed. Act and line references to Shakespeare's work are to the following:

Riverside	*The Riverside Shakespeare*, second edition, general editors, G. Blakemore Evans and J. J. M. Tobin (Boston, New York: Houghton Mifflin, 1997).
Chambers	E. K. Chambers, *William Shakespeare: A Study of Facts and Problems*. 2 vols. Oxford: Clarendon Press, 1930.
Dobson and Wells	*The Oxford Companion to Shakespeare*, edited by Michael Dobson and Stanley Wells. Oxford: Oxford University Press, 2001 [all references to the Stationers' Register are from this work].
First Folio	*Mr. William Shakespeares Comedies, Histories & Tragedies*. London: Isaac Jaggard, and Edward Blount, 1623. [References are to *The First Folio of Shakespeare*, edited by Charlton Hinman, New York: W. W. Norton, 1996 edition].
Foakes	*Henslowe's Diary*, second edition, edited by R. A. Foakes. Cambridge: Cambridge University Press, 2002 [all references to *Henslowe's Diary* are from this work].
Norton	*The Norton Shakespeare Based on the Oxford Edition*, second edition, edited by Stephen Greenblatt, Walter Cohen, Jean E. Howard, Katharine Eisaman Maus. New York, London: W. W. Norton & Co., 2008.

ODNB (online)   *Oxford Dictionary of National Biography* in
                   association with the British Academy from the
                   Earliest Times to the Year 2000 [and updates],
                   edited by H. G. C. Matthew, Brian Harrison
                   and Lawrence Goldman. Oxford: Oxford Uni-
                   versity Press and British Academy, 2004. Online
                   www.oxforddnb.com.

Schoenbaum   Samuel Schoenbaum, *Shakespeare's Lives*. New
                   Edition. Oxford: Clarendon Press, 1991.

Chapter One
Early Life: Birth, Upbringing, Family, Marriage. England at the Time

Birth and Stratford-upon-Avon

The name 'Gulielmus filius Johannes Shakespere' is recorded in the baptismal records in the parish register of Holy Trinity Church, Stratford-upon-Avon, Warwickshire on 26 April 1564. Tradition assigns the date of actual birth as 23 April 1564. This coincides with St. George's Day, that of the Patron Saint of England. Such a birth date also conveniently accords with Shakespeare's death 52 years later, on 23 April 1616.

William Shakespeare was the third child of John and Mary Shakespeare. They had a daughter named Joan who was baptized on 15 September 1558 but probably died at a very early age as his parents named another daughter Joan, who was christened in 1569. A Margaret Shakespeare was born in 1562 and died a year later. The parish register also records the christening of four other children: Gilbert, on 13 October 1566, he was buried in 1612; Anne, on 28 September 1571, buried in 1579; Richard, on 11 March 1574, died in 1613; and Edmund born on 3 May 1580. Edmund became a London-based actor, dying in 1607 and buried in what is today Southwark Cathedral. Joan married William Hart (d. 1616), who made hats in Stratford. She died in 1646, far outliving her famous brother William. Joan had three sons, each of whom inherited £5 in her brother's will and she was allowed to continue during her lifetime to live in the Shakespeare family property in Henley Street, Stratford.

The fact that his sisters – the first Joan, Margaret and Anne – either died in infancy or in early youth is some revelation of the fragility of existence during the last years of the sixteenth century. Indeed, Stratford and the surrounding districts were ravaged by a plague in the summer of 1564, the year Shakespeare was born. In fact, it is remarkable that the infant managed to survive a plague that probably killed one in eight of the population of Stratford in that year. According to Park Honan, 'In the late 1560s Stratford had only about a dozen streets, fewer than 240 households, and a populace (lately reduced by epidemic) of 1,200 people at most' (*Shakespeare: A Life*: 25). This was by no means an insignificant number. Coventry, then one of the largest of English towns and less than twenty miles from Stratford, had a population of between 7,000 and 8,000. Norwich, the largest population outside of London at the time, had less than 15,000 people, and London the capital too was perpetually beset by the plague. It is very difficult to speculate upon the actual size of its population and any estimate would be unreliable although an approximate figure of 200,000 has been given for the year 1600 (Dobson and Wells): 'Even in years spared by the plague, the number of deaths recorded in London's parish records always exceeded the live births' (Greenblatt, *Will in the World*: 163).

Parents

John Shakespeare: Father

Shakespeare's father, John, was probably born in or before 1530. He died in 1601. His family hailed from the village of Snitterfield near Stratford, where they were farmers. John was initially a craftsman, then a merchant and subsequently a glover. By April 1562, he had made enough money to buy a house and garden in the fashionable Henley Street and subsequently to acquire further property in Stratford. In 1556, he was sufficiently established locally to be trusted by the Stratford Council for the shared position as a taster of bread and ale. In April 1552, he paid a 12 pence fine for allowing dirt to pile up in front of his house. From 1561 to 1563, John served with a fellow town councillor as responsible for Stratford finances and property.

He became an alderman on 4 July 1565, and for a year from 1 October 1568, the bailiff or Mayor. It was during this period of service, in 1569, that the Queen's Men and Worcester's Men became the first professional acting company to perform in Stratford. Two years later, he was elected to the office of the Chief Alderman and Justice of the Peace. In January 1572, with a local dignitary named Adrian Quiney, he visited London on behalf of the town.

During these years, John steadily purchased property, for instance in 1575 paying £40 for the purchase of two Stratford houses with orchards and gardens. The surviving town records reveal that between 1568 and 1576, he attended every town council meeting. However, all was not well. For instance, around 1569, he was prosecuted for usury and sharp practices in wool-dealing. In 1570 and 1572, he was also accused, and in one case fined, for charging excessive interest on loans and for illegal wool purchases. By September 1586, John was replaced as an alderman for non-attendance at meetings. There were financial troubles. In late 1578, he was borrowing money by selling land, mortgaging some of his wife's inheritance and, in 1579, selling a share in the Snitterfield property. All this reflects the personal and economic uncertainties at the time, the ebb and flow of fortune so evident in his son's plays.

The record for John Shakespeare from 1584 is more difficult to establish as another John Shakespeare turns up in the Stratford records. The other John Shakespeare came from Warwick in 1584, was a shoemaker, lived in Bridge Street and married a local woman. A John Shakespeare appears on a 1592 list of Warwickshire recusants who failed to attend church or pay their debts. Whether or not Shakespeare's father was a recusant or secret Catholic has been the subject of considerable speculation. Clare Asquith argues in her *Shadowplay* that Shakespeare draws dramatically in his work upon his secret Catholic upbringing. For Asquith, the work is replete with coded messages relating to Catholicism and the dangers faced by Catholics in England: for instance, constancy in love being an allusion to fidelity to the old, true Catholic faith in Protestant England. E. A. J. Honigmann's *Shakespeare: The 'Lost Years'* (1998) argues that at one period of his youth, through family connections, Shakespeare was a schoolmaster, an actor for a prosperous Catholic Lancashire landowning family and that he was brought up as a Roman Catholic.

The waters are muddied as a good deal of the case seems to rest upon the apparent 1757 finding by a master bricklayer Joseph Mosely, during roof retiling in Stratford, of a now lost manuscript. This apparently was John Shakespeare's last will and testament. It was transcribed by John Jordan (1746–1809), a Stratford antiquarian. He sent a transcription to the Anglo-Irish scholar Edmond Malone (1741–1812). Malone invented an opening and transcribed the document, which is close to one circulating in the Midlands in the 1580s that had probably been written a decade earlier by Cardinal Carlo Borromeo (d. 1585), as a spiritual testament to the Catholic faith.

To return to the known, John Shakespeare's fortunes had revived sufficiently by 1596 for him to be granted a coat of arms. In other words, he became a gentleman of substance with 'lands and tenements of good wealth and substance' to be worth the then considerable sum of £500. Three years later, he applied to have his coat of arms integrated with those of his wife's family. Shakespeare's father died in 1601 and was buried on 8 September of that year (Chambers: I: 16).

Mary Arden (d. 1608): Shakespeare's Mother

John Shakespeare married into a wealthy family. His wife, Mary, was the youngest of the eight daughters of Robert Arden, a prosperous, well-connected farmer whose family owned land in Wilmcote, near Stratford. Robert was twice married, first to the mother of Mary. He subsequently remarried in 1548 a widow, the mother of two sons and two daughters from her first husband. Robert made his will on 24 November 1556. Mary, still unmarried at the time, was named as one of the two executors in addition to being left land on which to farm.

Mary probably married Shakespeare's father in 1557. Joan, their first child, was christened on 15 September 1558 and their last, Edmund, christened on 3 May 1580. Upon Mary's marriage, her valuable Wilmcote estate was passed over to her husband, who in times of subsequent financial crises did not hesitate to draw upon her inheritance in land and property. She died in 1608 being buried in Holy Trinity Church, Stratford, on 9 September 1608.

Shakespeare's Early Years and Schooling

There is no evidence that Shakespeare's parents could write, although signatures in the form of markings on documents are extant. It is assumed that from around the age of 5 to 7, Shakespeare attended a school where he would have learned to read. Stratford, in common with other English towns of a similar stature, had a grammar school, founded in 1427/8. The sons of prosperous town citizens probably then attended the King's New School. At this grammar school, they would have learned Latin literature, classical history, Livy, Cicero's speeches, Plautus's and Terence's comedies, Seneca's tragedies, Virgil's poetry and Ovid, a poet frequently referred to in Shakespeare's early work (see for instance *Love's Labour's Lost*: 4. 2. 122–5 and *As You Like It*, 3. 3. 8–9, and Dobson and Wells: 420, 120–124).

Studies of Elizabethan pedagogy reveal that emphasis was placed upon memory, composition and rhetoric. The opening scene of the fourth act of *The Merry Wives of Windsor* depicts a schoolmaster guiding a pupil named William through Latin grammar. School and compulsory church attendance would have resulted in a thorough knowledge of the *Bible* (probably the 1568 Bishops' Bible), the Book of Common Prayer (1549), and sermons in the *Book of Homilies* (published in 1571). There are biblical allusions throughout Shakespeare's works. Ecclesiastes and Job were special favourites. Passages in *Titus Andronicus* (4. 2. 43) and *Love's Labour's Lost* (4. 3. 336–337) reflect arguments concerning the translation of 'charity' or 'love'. The book of Job forms the biblical foundation of the abandonment by friends of someone whose luck has turned against them, for instance in *Timon of Athens*. Ecclesiastes is probably the source for the attack on excessive grief found in *Romeo and Juliet* and other plays. The title of *Measure for Measure* derives from Jesus's *Sermon on the Mount*: 'Judge not, that ye be not judged. For with what judgment ye judge, ye shall be judged, and with what measure ye mete, it shall be measured to you again' (*Mt.* 7.1–3: see N. Shaheen: 246–247).

'The Lost Years'

We do not know exactly when Shakespeare left school or what he did in his immediate post-school years. There is speculation.

The seventeenth-century antiquarian and biographer John Aubrey (1626–1697) notes that Shakespeare 'in his younger years [was] a schoolmaster in the country' (Schoenbaum: 59). It was customary to leave school at the age of 15. Other speculation relates to possible time spent in Lancashire with northern recusant relatives. There is mention in 1581 of one 'William Shakeshafte' in the will of a recusant from Lancashire, one Alexander de Hoghton. The problem with such evidence is that 'Shakeshafte', in spite of the different ways of spelling 'Shakespeare', comes close to it. Further, 'Shakeshafte' is a much more common name in Lancashire than in Warwickshire, so the connection is a very tenuous one (see Honigmann: 8–39, 141–142). A famous apocryphal tale concerning these years is that Shakespeare poached deer from Sir Thomas Lucy (1532–1600), who had an estate at Charlecote near Stratford. This story is first mentioned in a late seventeenth-century document.

Marriage, Anne Hathaway and Family

Whether Shakespeare was in Lancashire with a recusant family or not, he was back in Stratford by November 1582. On 27 November 1582, the 18-and-a-half-year old Shakespeare married Anne Hathaway (1555/6–1623), who was eight years older and three months pregnant. The sum of £40 was put up as a surety for the marriage as William was still technically a minor. He also required his father's approval of the marriage.

Anne Hathaway was one of seven children. Her father, Richard Hathaway (d. 1581), owned property and land, including the house known as 'Anne Hathaway's Cottage', an impressive residence that remained in the family until 1838. Shakespeare's father and Richard were not unacquainted, as the former acted as a guarantor for Richard and on two occasions settled his debts. The November 1582 marriage between Shakespeare's son and the late Richard's daughter was something of a shotgun affair. It took place after only one reading of the wedding banns rather than the customary three. They married at Temple Grafton, a village 5 miles west of Stratford. The vicar who married them, John Frith, was noted for his treatment of hawks but is described as 'unsound in religion' (Schoenbaum: 71).

The octosyllabic final couplet of Shakespeare's 145th sonnet contains an ambiguous pun on the name Hathaway:

'I hate' from the hate away she threw
And saved my life, saying 'not you'

Their first child, Susanna (Hall) Shakespeare (1583–1649), was baptized on 26 May 1583, six months after her parents' marriage. In May 1606, she refused to take Easter Holy Communion and married the Cambridge educated and staunchly Protestant physician Dr John Hall (*c*.1575–1635) on 5 June 1607. Her father for her marriage portion gave her 107 acres of land. They had one child, Elizabeth (1608–1670), and Shakespeare's will named the Halls as his executors. In fact, most of his property was left to Susanna, who died on 11 July 1649, outliving Charles I who was executed on 30 January 1649. Buried in Holy Trinity Church alongside her husband and near her parents, the inscription on her gravestone speaks of her wit:

Witty above her sex, but that's not all
Wise to salvation was good Mistress Hall,
Something of Shakespeare was in that.

Susanna's birth was followed by the baptism on 2 February 1585 of the twins Hamnet (1585–1596) and Judith (1585–1662). Shakespeare's only son was buried on 11 August 1596. It is thought that 'the Shakespeares named their twins after Hamnet Sadler, a young' Stratford baker 'and his wife Judith.' The Sadlers 'had lived in [Stratford] for many generations' (Schoenbaum: 12) and Hamnet, who also appears in local records under the name Hamlet, subsequently acted as a witness for Shakespeare's will. Judith lived an unusually long life for the times. She married Thomas Quiney (?1589–1662/1663), a tavern keeper on 10 February 1616, although less than six weeks later, he was prosecuted for 'incontinence' with a Margaret Wheeler, who had just been buried with a child. Shakespeare subsequently changed his will to protect Judith. She and Quiney had three sons, all of whom died at an early age.

New Place, one of the largest houses in Stratford, was purchased in May 1597 by Shakespeare, who bought it from the recusant

William Underhill (1555–1597). Underhill was poisoned by his eldest son, Fulke, who was subsequently executed in Warwick for the
crime. The spacious New Place seems to have been the first house
of their own that the Shakespeares lived in when he returned from
London, and he returned to it frequently owing to his numerous
local business transactions. It is probable that during her husband's
lengthy absences, Anne managed New Place. She is not recorded
as seeking poor relief, and no surviving signature of hers has been
discovered. There has been much speculation as to why she is not
mentioned directly in her husband's will. An added bequest leaves to
her his 'second best bed with the furniture'. Following his death, she
continued to live at New Place and legally was entitled a share in his
estate. Anne's gravestone is alongside her husband's. Below the mon-
ument to him in the Holy Trinity Church chancel is an inscription
attributed to her son-in-law John Hall: 'Heere lyeth interred the
body of Anne wife of William Shakespeare who departed this life the
6th day of August 1623 being of the age of 67 years.' This is followed
by six moving lines of Latin elegiacs. Translated, they mean:

> Breasts. Oh mother, milk and life thou didst give. Woe is me-for so
> great a boon shall I give stones? How much rather would I pray that
> the good angel should move the stone so that, like Christ's body,
> thine image might come forth! But my prayers are unavailing. Come
> quickly, Christ, that my mother though shut within this tomb, may
> rise again and seek the stars.
>
> (Dobson and Wells: 185).

Regrettably, far too little is known about Shakespeare's wife,
although the lack of hard evidence has not prevented speculation.
She has been the subject, for instance, of a brief novel by Robert
Nye, *Mrs. Shakespeare: The Complete Works* (1993), in which she
appears in London. Germaine Greer observes in her highly imaginative biography *Shakespeare's Wife* that 'most of Shakespeare's heroes
and heroines are motherless. The few mothers who do appear in
Shakespeare's plays are anything but motherly.' She instances Tamora
in *Titus Andronicus*, Juliet's neurotic mother in *Romeo and Juliet*,
Richard III's mother 'who curses her womb and the Countess of

Rossillion in *All's Well* who simply dislikes her son.' Greer adds, 'at best, mothers are ineffectual, like Queen Elizabeth in *Richard III*, Lady Falconbridge in *King John* and Lady Macduff, and at worst depraved, like Gertrude [in *Hamlet*] and Lady Macbeth' (Greer: 41).

General Historical Background

The well-known poet, dramatist and prose writer Robert Greene (1558–1592), in his *Greene's Groatsworth of Wit* (1592), mentions Shakespeare. We know consequently that by September 1592, when Greene died, Shakespeare was a force to be reckoned with on the London stage. Greene warns his fellow dramatists to be wary of the

> upstart crow, beautified with our feathers, that with his *Tyger's hart wrapped in a Player's hyde*, supposes he will be able to bombast out a blank verse as the best of you: and beeing an absolute *Iohannes fac totum* [Jack of all trades], is in his owne conceit the onely Shake-scene in a countrey. (McDonald, *The Bedford Companion*: 15)

There is here an allusion to the Duke of York's assault on Queen Margaret in *3 Henry VI*: 'O Tiger's heart wrapped in a woman's hide' (1, 4, 137).

Before turning to Shakespeare's theatrical activities in London from 1592 onwards, however, it is appropriate to reflect upon the state of the England into which he was born. Less than a century before Shakespeare's 1564 birth, years of bloody, intermittent feudal civil wars had terminated with the defeat and death, on the battlefield of Bosworth in Leicestershire, of Richard of York (1452–1485), Richard III, in 1485. He was defeated by Henry Tudor (1457–1509), the Earl of Richmond whose marriage to Elizabeth (1465–1503), daughter of Edward IV (1442–1483: reigned 1461–1483) united the warring dynastic factions of the houses of Lancaster and York.

Henry Tudor, Henry VII (reigned 1485–1509), thus created the Tudor dynasty. The Wars of the Roses, as these wars were known, form the background for Shakespeare's historical plays or tetralogies, starting with Richard II (1367–1400: reigned 1377–1399), who was deposed by Henry Bolingbroke, Henry IV (1367–1413: reigned 1399–1413), and they form the foundation for *Richard II* and the backcloth for *Henry IV: Parts 1 and 2*. Bolingbroke's son's foreign incursions form the settings for *Henry V* (1387–1422: reign 1413–1422). Henry V's relatively short reign left a void and a young heir, Henry VI (1422–1471: reigned 1422–1461). His reign was replete with internal instability and rebellion: these years are the subject matter for the three *Henry VI* plays, the product of Shakespeare's early years in London.

The defeat of Richard III and the beginnings of the Tudor dynasty resulted in some respite from the preceding years of instability, civil strife, bloodshed, rebellion and conspiracy. These are all concerns permeating Shakespeare's world. Indeed, the fear of chaos is prevalent: 'take but degree away, untune that string | and hark what discord follows' (*Troilus and Cressida* 1. 3. 109. 110), expressed in a musical metaphor, conveys the dramatist's excessive fear of a lack of authority and the need for control and order. Apart from an appearance in *Richard III*, Henry Tudor is not a major character in a Shakespeare play. His son who succeeded him in 1509, Henry VIII (1491–1547), is the main focus of what is generally taken to be a late collaborative work, *All Is True* (*Henry VIII*) featuring Cardinal Wolsey, Thomas Wolsey (*c.*1475–1530). Wolsey played a major role in Henry's regime, helping with the execution of Edward Stafford (1478–1521), the 3rd Duke of Buckingham, who was usurping too much power at court. Wolsey also played a major part in advising Henry to divorce his first wife, Katherine of Aragon (1485–1536).

The attention is on domestic court politics rather than on civil war and bloody civil strife. However, Henry's divorce had traumatic religious ramifications because of his break with Rome, with Papal supremacy, Catholicism and the creation of the Church of England. All this was done to divorce Katherine and marry, in the first instance, Anne Boleyn (*c.*1507–1536), the second of his six wives, and to secure a male heir for the throne. Anne was beheaded on charges of alleged adultery, slightly less than three years after giving birth to a daughter, Elizabeth (1532–1603), who subsequently became the great Queen Elizabeth I (1558–1603). The ideological framework for the break with Rome, known as the English Reformation, was spearheaded by Thomas Cranmer (1489–1556), who as Archbishop of Canterbury crowned Anne.

The break with Rome – the assertion of national supremacy against Papal foreign interference – played itself out in various areas of domestic life. For instance, Henry VIII's appropriation of the church's vast resources, the destruction of its property, revenues and confiscation of its lands, was carried out in the Dissolution of the Monasteries from 1536–1540: the monasteries had become, to use the evocative words of Sonnet 73, 'Bare ruined choirs, where late the sweet birds sang'. The chief executioner for this was Thomas Cromwell (1485–1540), Henry's leading minister and formerly secretary to Cardinal Wolsey. Cromwell himself did not outlive his Master, being executed on a charge of treason in 1540. Henry VIII's court and political intrigues form the background for the manuscript *Sir Thomas More*, a part of which is attributed to Shakespeare and centres upon the figure of Sir Thomas More (1478–1535), Lord Chancellor from 1529 to 1534, who refused to recognize his monarch's marriage to Anne Boleyn or to sign the Act of Supremacy that made Henry the Supreme Head of the Church of England. These acts of defiance resulted in his execution.

Shortly following Anne Boleyn's execution, Henry VIII married her serving lady Jane Seymour (1508/1509–1537). Never officially crowned, as the coronation was delayed due to one of the periodic outbreaks of the plague in London, Jane fulfilled her duty by giving birth to a son and heir. Edward (1537–1553) succeeded his father to the throne as Edward VI in 1547 at the tender age of just over nine. His mother died from the complications of childbirth: when Henry died, he was buried beside her, although he had three subsequent wives. Anne of Cleves (1515–1557), whom he married in 1540, was the consequence of a Protestant political alliance. She was not to Henry's taste and the marriage was quickly annulled, its chief victim probably being Thomas Cranmer, who on political grounds conducted the marital negotiations.

The penultimate wife, Catherine Howard (*c.*1520/1525–1542), was descended from the Howards, an eminent Catholic aristocratic family. She had a somewhat checkered past and was beheaded less than two years after the marriage on charges of treason and adultery. Catherine Parr (*c.*1512–1548), who had already seen two previous husbands and also came from an aristocratic background, was the sixth and final wife. She remarried following Henry's death, dying in childbirth in 1548. None of these later wives form the foundation for a Shakespeare play. Maybe the subject was far too sensitive, as they belong to Henry VIII's last disease-ridden years and he was, after all, the father of Elizabeth I.

The chorus at the conclusion of *Henry V* notes that 'Henry the sixth, in infant bands crowned king . . . did this king succeed | Whose state so many had the managing.' These words may be applied to the tumultuous years following Henry VIII's death in 1547. His young son lasted but six years, during which power transferred hands regularly in political infighting at court and rebellion. Most of his advisors were staunch Protestants who pushed through religious reforms such as the 1549 Act of Uniformity prescribing Protestant rights for services and imposing the use of Cranmer's Book of Common Prayer. Edward VI was followed by Mary I (1516–1558), the daughter of Henry VIII's first wife Katherine of Aragon. A devout Catholic, Mary Tudor (1553–1558), partly in an effort to reconcile England with the emerging powerful country of Spain on the European mainland, and largely to secure a Catholic heir for the English throne and to fully restore English Catholicism, married King Philip of Spain (1527–1598) in 1554.

Mary attempted to overturn the Protestant reforms of her half-brother's reign and to reinstate Catholicism. Cranmer was executed and replaced by Reginald Cardinal Pole (1500–1558), who led the Counter-Reformation against the Church of England. Henry VIII's religious laws were repealed. The Marian persecutions against Protestants proceeded apace, and it is estimated that just under 300 were burnt at the stake for their religious beliefs, leaving a legacy of great bitterness.

Henry VIII in 1542 created the Kingdom of Ireland. This was reconfirmed by Mary in 1555. She and Philip managed to obtain Papal consent for this and English colonial settlements in Ireland. She attempted, too, to involve England in the Spanish campaign against France. Indeed, in January 1558, an English army lost control of Calais, the only possession remaining in France from Henry V's invasion. In the meantime, the economic situation went from bad to worse, and the country failed to benefit from the expanding New World trade.

Mary left no heir; she died in 1558 and was succeeded by her half-sister, who became Elizabeth I. This was the world into which

Shakespeare was born almost six years later. Very much a child of the Elizabethan age, Shakespeare's work largely reflects in one form or another, the specific difficulties the new monarch Elizabeth inherited. There was the problem of securing the throne; she did this through choosing the right trusted advisors. There was the religious problem. On her ascendancy, the church of her father, the Church of England, was restored and under the guidance of a powerful Archbishop of Canterbury Matthew Parker (1504–1575) a new translation of the *Bible* was published, the Bishops' Bible, in 1568. Other religious changes included the 1571 Act of Uniformity, which required English Catholics to relinquish allegiance to Rome and join the English Church.

In foreign and economic affairs, Spain was gaining ascendancy and fermenting internal discontent in England through encouraging Catholic revivalism and dissent, and stirring up trouble in Scotland, in Ireland and on the high seas. France and the Lowlands were in turmoil. In an extremely difficult terrain, Elizabeth and her advisors needed to tread very carefully. The abortive 1588 attempted invasion by the Spanish Armada did not help matters, strengthening English national feeling and acerbating anti-Spanish and anti-Catholic sentiments. Elizabeth's internal intelligence agents were on the lookout for recusants owing allegiance to a foreign power and tortured on the rack those alleged to be treasonous. Naturally parsimonious, Elizabeth and her advisors ran a very tight economic ship. She encouraged individual naval enterprise, the merchant adventurers, inevitably leading to further conflict with Spain on the high seas. Rebellions were crushed in Ireland and resettlement in the country proceeded apace.

Resisting marriage, Elizabeth had many favourites. Two in particular were the Earl of Leicester and the Earl of Essex. Robert Dudley, Earl of Leicester (?1532–1588), was extremely well connected, and a known Protestant. At one time, he was suggested as a second husband for Mary, Queen of Scots, Mary Stuart (1542–1587), who was executed for treason after being involved in one way or another with three assassination attempts on Elizabeth. From 1564 until his death, Dudley became Elizabeth's official protector as the Earl of Leicester. The relationship was a tempestuous one; Leicester acquired a reputation of being a lady's man. He was placed in command of a 1585 campaign in the Netherlands and was responsible for the English land forces against the 1588 Spanish Armada. Elizabeth was devastated by his subsequent death.

He was succeeded in her affections by his stepson, Robert Devereux, 2nd Earl of Essex (1566–1601). Married to the daughter of Sir Francis Walsingham (*c.*1532–1590), Elizabeth's first spymaster and trusted advisor, Essex's great-grandmother Mary was the sister of Anne Boleyn, the mother of Elizabeth. Tempestuous at court, he alienated the very powerful Sir Robert Cecil (Lord Burghley 1563–1612), Elizabeth's chief statesman, minister and espionage chief. Ignoring the Queen's orders, he participated in an unsuccessful attempt to take Lisbon following the defeat of the Armada. In 1596, he captured Cadiz, but a year later, he again defied orders by pursuing the Spanish treasure ships without making sure that the Spanish navy was crippled. Placed, by his express request, in charge of an Irish campaign in 1599, he failed, and led a rebellion in London against Elizabeth. Cecil was instrumental in ordering his subsequent execution.

Discontent, rebellion, treason, treachery and death pervade Shakespeare's dramas. Some eminent literary scholars and critics have seen resemblances between Shakespeare's Hamlet and Essex. In the words of John Dover Wilson (1881–1969) in his *The Essential Shakespeare: A Biographical Adventure* (1932) the Globe Theatre performance of *Richard II* the day before Essex' uprising took place 'With a view to inciting the people against the queen and showing them that sovereigns had been deposed and might be again.' For Dover Wilson, 'Hamlet is not Essex, he is Shakespeare's effort to understand Essex, to understand him as a dramatist' (102–104). Yet it is not speculation that Elizabeth, in common with her favourites, loved the theatre.

Chapter Two
London: The Elizabethan Stage, the Early History Plays

London

The London of 1592 where Shakespeare had, according to his fellow dramatist and rival Robert Greene, already become known, was the capital of the country and an ever-expanding city. In spite of high mortality rates, immigration into London and its environs from elsewhere in England was on the increase. John Stow (1525–1605) records in his *Survey of London* (1598, 1603) that between December 1592 and the following December, 11,000 people in London out of approximately 200,000 died owing to the plague. Indeed, outbreaks of the plague were a common occurrence. Rats or fleas – considered by modern medical authorities to be the chief causes, in addition to unsatisfactory sanitation, lack of drainage and primitive refuge disposal – were not considered then as the main causes. Plagues were attributed to contagion in the air and spread by those already suffering from illness. Crowds were to be avoided; consequently the theatres where crowds gathered were closed. Between the years 1603 and 1613, the total theatrical closures due to the plague accumulated to a grand total of 78 months.

London had its very wealthy and its very poor. The controlling elite depended on its business transactions, land ownership and court connections. Trade with the European continent, especially the wool and cloth industries, expanded, bringing with it immigration from abroad in addition to internal migration from parts of what became the British Isles and Ireland. It is estimated that more than 20 per cent of the population of London was involved in some manner or another in the manufacture of clothes.

London, too, was the political, financial and cultural centre of the country. It was also an area of poverty, disease and the mob, often unruly and out of control. The poverty, a rootless shifting population and its dangers is reflected in the 1572 Act for the Punishment of Vagabonds, the most severe of the many Tudor Poor Laws. Included in the act as rogues, vagabonds and beggars were bear wardens and players – in other words, actors. If convicted of any of these so-called offences the penalty was whipping and having a hot compass iron roughly of about an inch in length bored through the right ear gristle. A second conviction meant condemnation as a felon, and a third conviction resulted in execution with the removal of whatever land and property might be possessed.

It is not surprising that London was a place of violence. During the years 1581–1602, at least 35 riots were recorded: 12 of these took place in June 1595. There were protests against a most unpopular Lord Mayor, Sir John Spencer (d. 1610), riots against foreigners and efforts to free prisoners. Various forms of riots are depicted in Shakespeare's plays: in *Coriolanus* there is a populist uprising; Jack Cade leads a popular uprising in *Henry VI, Part 2*; there is mob violence in *Julius Caesar* and a personal rebellion or 'riotous head' by Laertes in *Hamlet* (4. 5. 102). Riots were by no means confined to London. There were regular rural disturbances in opposition to commons and waste land enclosures by local land owners or in the royal forests by the crown. The violence in these instances was not directed at persons but aimed at property. For instance, villagers gathered to destroy freshly planted hedges and vegetation. Such protests were accompanied by extensive drinking bouts.

During Shakespeare's lifetime in Stratford-upon-Avon in January 1601, his friend Richard Quiney (before 1577–1602), the author of the only surviving letter addressed to Shakespeare, one requesting a large sum of money, was involved in a riot. Quiney and others destroyed the hedges and other property of Sir Edward Greville, a local Lord. Subsequently, Quiney died from a blow to the head from one of Greville's men during a tavern brawl. Further, in January 1615 near Stratford-upon-Avon, there was physical opposition to the filling in of a ditch by one William Combe, who was enclosing common land near to the town (see Chambers: II: 148; I: 183).

The Elizabethan Stage

The growth of London led to an increase in prostitution, brothels, animal baiting – a most popular activity – and theatres. There was a long tradition of theatre in England; for instance, late medieval England witnessed in many towns annual festivals mounting cycles of dramas depicting the biblical stories from Adam and Eve to the Passion of Jesus. The York miracle plays are probably the best known. It is somewhat surprising that it was not until at least 1567 that mention is made of an initial 'permanent freestanding public' theatre (*Norton*: 30). The Red Lion in London was named in 1567. In 1576, The Theatre was built for James Burbage (*c*.1531–1597). By the time Shakespeare is noticed as being in London in 1592, there was a very active London theatrical life. The Red Lion in Stepney had a single-story gallery and a 40-feet-by-30-feet and 5-feet high stage, plus a turret protruding 30 feet above ground level. There do not appear to have been solid foundations implanted at ground level. Burbage's theatre was erected in Shoreditch, then on the outskirts of London. Nearby was Henry Lanham's Curtain Theatre (Dobson and Wells: 99) erected in 1577. Both were similar to the circular design found in Roman amphitheatres.

Other notable theatres include Richard Farrant's (*c*.1528–1580) use of the Black Friar's Dominican Monastery in 1576. Archaeological exploration at the end of the twentieth century revealed the foundations and design of the Rose Theatre in London's south bank close to the more famous Globe Theatre associated with Shakespeare. In 1989, building workers demolishing an office building by accident uncovered the foundations of the Rose. This theatre was initially built in 1587 and enlarged by the theatrical entrepreneur Philip Henslowe (1555/6–1616) in 1592. Indeed, a good deal of our knowledge of London Elizabethan theatrical activity during the last decades of the sixteenth century and early seventeenth century comes from him.

Excavations and Henslowe's evidence reveal that the Rose was spatially a 14-sided, irregular polygon measuring approximately 74 feet across, with a small stage that tapered in front or created a chord across three auditorium bays. A 1592 enlargement was in the yard space. A stage cover and stage posts also belong to the 1592 alteration or were created subsequently. The roof was thatched and there was a rain water erosion area in the yard. Henslowe's papers reveal that plays by Christopher Marlowe (1564–1593), Thomas Kyd (1558–1594), the early George Chapman (1559–1639), Thomas Heywood (*c*.1570s–1641) and Thomas Dekker (1572–1632), were performed between 1594 and 1600 by a permanent company for large profits. The 1592 enlargement was made primarily for Henslowe's star attraction, the actor Edward Alleyn (1566–1616).

Theatre companies and the performers attracted patrons. Alleyn's surviving correspondence shows that he was connected as an actor very early on with the Worcester's Men associated with the Earl of Worcester. In 1569, Shakespeare's father as the Stratford bailiff approved the payments of 12d (pence) to them for a performance at Stratford. More importantly, Alleyn was a member of the highly prestigious Admiral/Prince Henry's men between 1589 and 1597 and again between 1600 and 1606. These became the main rivals of Shakespeare's company and owed allegiance to Charles Howard, 2nd Lord Effingham (1536–1624), who in 1585 became Lord Admiral and, in 1597, the Earl of Nottingham; he had royal connections.

Alleyn was noted for his performances in Marlowe's dramas. On 22 October 1592, he married Henslowe's step-daughter Joan Woodward (d. 1623), so in other words, he married into the business. Thomas Nashe (1567–*c*.1601), a powerful figure in the London dramatic world at the time, in 1592 referred to Alleyn as the greatest tragedian of the period. Alleyn also wore the Admiral's livery or clothing. In May 1594, the Lord Chamberlain, a very powerful court official responsible for directing and controlling the theatres, made changes in the London theatres. At the time, the Chamberlain was Henry Carey, Lord Hunsdon (1526–1596), who was patron of Shakespeare's acting company created in 1594. His mistress was Emilia Lanier (1569–1645), the possible 'Dark Lady' of the Sonnets. Carey was succeeded by William Brooke, 7th Lord Cobham (d. 1597), a descendant of Sir John Oldcastle (d. 1417), a Lollard martyr and the basis for Shakespeare's Falstaff. Cobham objected to the treatment of his ancestor in *Henry IV, Part I*. Following Cobham's death in March 1597, George Carey, 2nd Lord Hunsdon (1547–1603) who supported the Chamberlain's Men became Lord Chamberlain.

The May 1594 theatrical redistribution placed the best actors from their previous companies into two fresh units; one was under the patronage of the Lord Chamberlain and the other controlled by his son-in-law, the Lord Admiral. Only these two companies were allowed London performances at specifically assigned theatres. One of these, the Admiral's, was the Rose with Alleyn, south of the River Thames. The other was north of the river, the Chamberlain's Men. This was the company with which Shakespeare was associated.

The years 1592–1594 were difficult ones. The plague led to a lengthy closure of all of the London theatres and, by the end of 1593, many of the companies were near collapse. The May 1594 redistribution consolidated the London theatres. No doubt the Lord Chamberlain's motives were mixed, as much to secure the actors for the court audience as for a general London audience. So Alleyn and the Rose were to all intents and purposes one company in the post-1594 London theatrical world. The other company, the Chamberlain's men under the Lord Chamberlain Henry Carey, occupied the playhouse across the Thames. This was James Burbage's theatre. Burbage was an eminent woodworker and theatre constructor who also acted. His son, Richard Burbage (1568–1619), became the leading performer in Shakespeare's company whose star was in the ascendancy following the 1594 settlement of the Chamberlain's Men at his father's theatre. There is a record of a 15 March 1595 payment to Shakespeare, Will Kempe, the comic actor (d. 1603) and Burbage for court performances in December 1594.

The Rose and Burbage's theatre were competitors. There were other theatres, too. The Curtain was built in Holywell in 1577. The Swan, built in Southwark in 1595, did not see much usage. It was, however, the subject of a 1596 visit by Johannes de Witt, the Dutch humanist scholar who drew it. His friend Amout van Buchel copied it and his 'sketch is the only surviving interior view of an open-air playhouse of the period.' It reveals an almost 'round amphitheatre of between 16 and 24 sides with a stage projecting into the yard surmounted by a stage cover supported on two pillars' (Dobson and

Wells: 457). The Swan was closed in 1597 following a performance by the Earl of Pembroke's Men of a now lost play by Thomas Nashe and Ben Jonson (1572–1637), *The Isle of Dogs*. This performance so openly criticized the existing power structures that the dramatists were imprisoned. Evidence from Marlowe's plays and others suggests that the theatres consisted of a platform stage; there were two stage pillars, a trap door and probably some kind of 'flying mechanism in the stage cover' (Gurr: 6).

James Burbage's theatre was dismantled shortly after Christmas 1598 and replaced by the Globe, built from its scaffolding and remains. It was situated in an area of south London, along the Thames, Bankside, noted for its brothels and animal-baiting rings. Open-aired, almost circular, an amphitheatre consisting of a thatched roof and a diameter between eight and one hundred feet, it witnessed performances of at the very least seventeen of the greatest of Shakespeare's plays. These range from *As You Like It*, *Julius Caesar*, and *Hamlet* to *The Winter's Tale*. It was burnt down on 29 June 1613 during a performance of Shakespeare and his collaborator's *Henry VIII*.

Unlike other theatres operated by entrepreneurs, the Globe was run by a group of its leading players, the Chamberlain's Men. Shakespeare put up 10 percent of the costs for the transformation of the theatre into the Globe. The leading players were also the shareholders or 'housekeepers' of their own theatre. The excavations of 1989 and subsequently reveal that the Globe had 20 sides, turret stairway connected to a section of outer wall and an interior gallery wall. In 1997, a reconstruction officially opened with a production of *Henry V* with Mark Rylance (b. 1960) in the leading role.

Shakespeare's Early Dramas

Probably the three *Henry VI* plays belong to the earliest period of Shakespeare's dramatic output. As we have seen, Robert Greene quotes from *Henry VI, Part 3*. Another contemporary, Francis Meres (1565/6–1647), wrote *Palladis Tamia: Wit's Treasury. Being the Second Part of Wit's Commonwealth*, registered at Stationer's Register on 7 September 1598. It refers to Shakespeare's 'sugared Sonnets among his private friends' and divides Shakespeare's work into two main genres. There is 'Comedy' and included in this category are *The Two Gentlemen of Verona*, *The Comedy of Errors*, *Love's Labour's Lost*, *A Midsummer Night's Dream*, *The Merchant of Venice* and *Love's Labour's Won*, a play now lost although a Quarto title page was seen and it is listed in the bookseller's catalogue dated August 1603. Under the category of 'Tragedy', Meres lists *Richard II*, *Richard III*, the two *Henry IV* plays, *King John*, *Titus Andronicus* and *Romeo and Juliet*.

The Early Histories

The catalogue 'of the [several] Comedies, Histories, and Tragedies Contained in This Volume' included in the preliminary matter to the *First Folio* (1623) of Shakespeare's works lists amongst his 'Histories' *King John*, *Richard II*, *Henry IV, Parts I and II*, *Henry V*, the three *Henry VI* plays, *Richard III* and *Henry VIII*. In other words, those dealing with the Wars of the Roses and a late play dealing with Elizabeth I's father. Characteristic features of these plays are that they all deal with traumatic periods of English history, as opposed to Roman, Greek or even French history. They are concerned with periods of change and transition that have contemporary reverberations for Shakespeare's audience. The 1590s were an unsettling time. The reigning monarch was not getting younger; there were no obvious heirs, she was childless; she was unmarried; rebellion and dissent were in the air. Externally, Spain licked its wounds as an injured tiger recovering from the ignominy of the Spanish Armada debacle; and France and the Netherlands were in turmoil. Common to the history plays are the themes of patriotism, the fear of treason, the dominant concern of who will inherit the throne and the issue of the Divine Right of a monarch to rule as if the monarch were the lord's anointed. Such a belief creates profound unease and a troubled conscience for the slayer of Richard II – Henry IV. The enactment of chaos, anarchy, and its consequences pervades these histories and other Shakespearean drama.

The Histories owe much to the Chronicle plays. Ralph Holinshed's (d. *c*.1580) *Chronicles of England, Scotland and Ireland* (1577, 1587) provides crucial source materials utilized by Shakespeare and other contemporary dramatists in their historical chronicle dramas.

The *Chronicles* are the product of many hands and reflect differing and at times conflicting views of similar events. The ambiguity is reflected, too, in Shakespeare, for instance in the final Chorus's speech of *Henry V*. The chorus speaks of Henry's glory, as does Holinshed, but then speaks of the human cost of the French war, since 'so many had the managing' of his young son's estate 'that they lost France and made his England bleed' (5. 3. 11–12).

To return to the *Chronicles*, as drama in the period after the 1588 defeat of the Spanish Armada, their nationalist focus and patriotic emphasis may explain their popularity. Theatrically, they depicted episodic series of events during the reign of an English monarch. Common features are staged spectacles such as the funeral of Henry V that opens *Henry VI, Part I*, pageantry and battle scene after battle scene depicting the flow of conflict and the changing fortunes of the battlefield. Scholarship at the start of the twenty-first century, assisted by computer word cluster searches, suggest that drama previously solely attributed to Shakespeare was also written by others. Brian Vickers (b. 1937) attributes to Thomas 'Kyd authorship of about two-thirds of *1 Henry VI*' (*Letters*, *TLS*, May 14, 2008: 6). In other words, authorship teams were at work, with one dramatist contributing say one scene, and others additional parts of the play. Thomas Kyd is but one of the dramatists who worked with Shakespeare.

Philip Henslowe noted in his diary on 3 March 1592 a new performance of 'Harry VI'(Dobson and Wells: 200). Box office receipts set a record for the theatrical season and over a ten-month period the play was performed at least fifteen times. Thomas Nashe in his *Piers Penilesse His Supplication to the [Devil]* (mid 1592) draws upon the model of the war hero in *Henry VI, Part I* to defend the theatre against attacks on the grounds of morality:

> How would it have ioyed braue *Talbot* (the terror of the French) to thinke that after he had lyne two hundred yeares in his Tombe, hee should triumphe againe on the Stage, and haue his bones newe embalmed with the teares of ten thousand spectators at least, (at seuerall times) who, in the Tragedian that represents his person, imagine they behold him fresh breeding? (cited Chambers: II: 188).

Of course, Nashe may well have been biased as he possibly had a hand, with at least a couple of other dramatists, in the writing of the play.

The text of *Henry VI, Part I* is found in the 1623 *First Folio*. The second part was published in a Quarto version, that is the publication of a Shakespeare text as a separate single entity in book format 'in which the sheets are printed for folding twice, each sheet . . . producing four leaves (eight pages)'. This differs from the Folio or the first collected edition. A Folio is 'a book formed in which sheets are printed for folding once, each sheet thus producing two leaves (four pages)' (Williams and Abbot:157, 147). The Quarto version (Q1) appeared in 1594 with the title *The First Part of the Contention of the Two Famous Houses of York and Lancaster*. Quarto versions also were published in 1600 and 1619. In the *First Folio* (F1), it appeared under the title *The Second Part of Henry VI*. Some modern editions, including *The Norton Shakespeare Based on the Oxford Edition* (1997), use the Quarto title.

The third part of the trilogy was published individually in 1595 under the title *The True Tragedy of Richard Duke of York, with the Death of Good King Henry the Sixth with the Whole Contention between the Two Houses Lancaster and York*. It focuses upon attempts by a rival Yorkist to seize the throne from the weak Henry IV. The Yorkists are led by Richard of York, who at the conclusion of the first act is killed. He leaves four sons, one of whom, Richard, eventually Duke of Gloucester, is obsessed with gaining the throne. In addition to battles and spectacles in the manner of the Chronicle plays, there are passages of powerful poetry (see for instance 5. 6. 78–84).

Chapter Three
The Poems and Sonnets

Venus and Adonis

By 1594, William Shakespeare was an established dramatist on the London stage. The first of Shakespeare's works to appear in print is the 1,194-line narrative poem *Venus and Adonis*. Published as a Quarto in 1593, some evidence of its popularity lies in the fact that only one copy seems to have survived, a copy in the Bodleian Library, Oxford. The Stationers' Register, where all publications were entered as the Stationers' had a monopoly of paper distribution, enters the publication on 18 April 1593. According to another contemporary record, it was being sold by 21 September. The printer was a fellow Stratfordian, Richard Field, born in Stratford in 1562. Field also printed *The Rape of Lucrece* in the following year.

Venus and Adonis was probably Shakespeare's most popular published work. Between 1593 and 1636, it went through sixteen editions and was frequently alluded to in the works of others. Probably its popularity was due to its blatant erotic content. *Venus and Adonis* is dedicated in a fulsome manner to 'To The Right Honourable Henry Wriothesley, Earl of Southampton, and Baron of Titchfield.' Before the dedication is a citation from Ovid's *Amores*: 'Let vile people admire vile things; may fair-haired Apollo serve me goblets filled with Castalian [sacred to the Muses] water' (1. 15. 35–36). Shakespeare here shows familiarity with the work of the great Roman poet Publius Ovidius Naso (43BC–AD17) and the erotic love poems, the *Amores*, of his favourite classical poet. There are complimentary references to Ovid in, for instance, *Love's Labour's Lost* (4. 2. 122–125) and *As You Like It* (3. 3. 5–6), and Ovid is a major source for *The Rape of Lucrece*. Apollo, the god of poetry, is also alluded to frequently (see for instance

The Taming of the Shrew, Induction. 2. 34. 58) and *Love's Labour's Lost* (4. 3. 319).

The Earl of Southampton

Henry Wriothesley (1573–1624), a highly connected 19-year-old Aristocrat, is the dedicatee. The humble poet writes: 'I know not how I shall offend in dedicating my unpolished lines to your lordship, nor how the world will censure me for choosing so strong a prop to support so weak a burden.' His aim is to please the young Earl with 'the first heir of my invention'. If it 'prove deformed, I shall be sorry it had so noble a godfather, and never after eare', or cultivate 'so barren a land for fear it yield me still [always] so bad a harvest'. The reference to 'the first heir of my invention' refers to *Venus and Adonis* 'implicitly contrasting this legitimate venture into verse on a classical subject with' the author's 'illegitimate earlier work for the stage' (Dobson and Wells: 510).

Southampton was a patron of the arts and frequenter of the playhouses. A contemporary, Rowland Whyte, describes him in 1600 as passing 'away the time in London merely going to two plays every day.' A contemporary portrait in an unknown hand reproduced in the *ODNB (online)* reveals him to be a most impressive figure, with a mane of hair, eminently fashionable clothing, decorated gloves, within the background a black and white cat looking somewhat quizzical!

Robert Cecil, Elizabeth I's most powerful minister, Secretary of State (1596–1608) and the object of the abortive 1601 Essex Rebellion, planned in 1590 a marriage between his 17-year-old granddaughter, Elizabeth Vere, and the Earl of Southampton, who refused the match. In 1595, Southampton married a lady-in-waiting of Elizabeth I, Elizabeth Vernon, after she became pregnant. Both incurred the queen's wrath and were briefly imprisoned. The reluctance to marry is one of the topics of the first 17 sonnets, and Southampton is one of the chief candidates for the 'Fair Youth' of the sonnets.

At court, Southampton was closely associated with Robert Devereux, the Earl of Essex, and was implicated in Essex's disastrous, tragic 1601 rebellion against the Queen. As a consequence, Southampton was imprisoned but released upon James I's succession to the throne in 1603. On 5 February 1601, Southampton sent the relatively large sum of 40 shillings to Shakespeare's Globe Company with a request for a revival of *Richard II*. The history focusing on the deposing of the monarch, the lord's anointed, with its emphasis on the concept of the Divine Right of Kings, probably had relevance to Essex's rebellion. Upon release from imprisonment, Southampton's fortunes were restored and, he became involved with overseas colonial ventures, participating for instance in the Virginia Company. One of its ships, *The Sea Adventure*, was wrecked off Bermuda in 1609 and probably provided the background for *The Tempest*.

The Rape of Lucrece

Whether or not Southampton was Shakespeare's patron by 1593 is open to question. Possibly the fulsome dedication to *Venus and Adonis* is a plea for support. Southampton was the patron of Thomas Nashe and the half-Italian John Florio (?1554–?1625), subsequently noted for his translations, especially of Montaigne (1533–1592) from the French, and owner of a famed library. Shakespeare fulsomely dedicated *The Rape of Lucrece*, his poem dealing with rape and suicide, to Southampton. 'The love I dedicate to your lordship is without end . . . [w]hat I have done is yours; what I have to do is yours; being part in all I have, devoted yours.' The poem appears in the Stationers' Register in May 1594 under the title *The Ravishment of Lucrece* and was published as a Quarto in the same year. Although not achieving the popular success of *Venus and Adonis*, the poem drawing upon Ovid, in this instance his historical *Fasti* or Chronicles, focused upon the acquisition through murder of kingship, the consequences of rape and a republican rebellion, went through various editions, contemporary allusions and imitations.

The Sonnets

First published in their entirety in 1609, the sonnets have a curious dedication. This reads, 'To the onlie begetter of these ensuing sonnets Mr. W. H. all happinesse and that eternite promised by our ever-living poet wisheth the well-wishing adventurer in setting forth. T.T.' (Thomas Thorpe [active 1584–1625], the printer, 'the well-wishing adventurer'). Whether or not the initials 'W. H.' are Henry Wriothesley (the Earl of Southampton) in reverse or a printer's error has been the subject of much speculation.

The dating of the 154 sonnets, too, has been the subject of much debate. Francis Meres in his *Palladus Tamia* of 1598, observes, 'The sweet witty soul of Ovid lies in mellifluous and honey-tongued Shakespeare, witness his *Venice and Adonis*, his *Lucrece*, his sugared sonnets among his private friends, &c.' In the same year, the poet Richard Barnfield (1574–1627) in his *Lady Pecunia* praises the 'honey flowing vein' of Shakespeare's sonnets. Barnfield wrote two distinct homoerotic verse collections, *The Affectionate Shepherd* (1594) and a year later, *Cynthia* (1595). So although not published in their entirety until 1609, Shakespeare's sonnets were extolled at least a decade before their publication. Two sonnets, 138 and 144, are printed in the second edition of a collection of 20 brief poems attributed to Shakespeare, *The Passionate Pilgrim*, published in 1599 by William Jaggard (1591–1623). Jaggard, subsequently with his son Isaac (d. 1627), was to print the *First Folio*. *The Passionate Pilgrim* also includes three extracts from *Love's Labour's Lost* in addition to poems by others. In terms of subject matter, there appears to be a critical consensus that Sonnets 1–126 are an account of the speaker's complicated relationship or love for an effeminate, attractive, aristo-cratic young man. The initial 17 sonnets are addressed to the 'Fair Youth' and urge him to get married and produce an heir. Sonnets 78–80 and 82–86 reveal a poetic competitor for his affections, and there is a love triangle revealed in Sonnets 40–42. Sonnets 87–90 are laments: 'Farewell, thou are too dear for my possessing' (87), regrets that the poet has been forgotten, 'When thou shalt be dispos'd to set me light' (88). However, Sonnets 91–96 indicate some kind of resto-ration in the relationship, and 117–120 suggest infidelity on the poet's part: 'So I return rebuk'd to my content' (119).

Sonnets 127–152 are regarded as the bitter sonnets preoccupied with 'black beauty's successive heir' (127), the dark non-aristocratic lady: 'Thou art as tyrannous, so as thou art' (131). Sonnet 126, with its opening 'O thou, my lovely boy, who in thy power | Dost hold Time's fickle glass, his sickle, hour', a 12-line rather than 14-line sonnet, is perceived as a transition mark, as the final poem addressed to the aristocratic young man. The second line contains the admonishment that the boy, too, will be subject to time. Indeed, time, mutability, is one of the great repetitive motifs in the sonnets and throughout Shakespeare's work. It does, however, lead the poet to moments of hubris. For instance, in Sonnet 18 beginning, 'Shall I compare thee to a Summers day?' utilizing imagery drawn from nature, the 'rough winds', 'the darling buds of May', legal imagery so common in Shakespeare's work, 'summer's lease hath all to short a date,' he tells the addressee, the subject of the poem that he/she will live on as long as the poem does: 'Nor shall Death brag thou wand'rest in his shade, | When in eternal lines to time thou grow'st'.

Many of Shakespeare's sonnets are regarded as among his very finest work and they have stood the test of time. Throughout the centuries, they have meant many things to a great many people, different people from diverse backgrounds. For instance, the great nineteenth-century English novelist George Eliot (Marian Evans, 1819–1880) wrote out lines from the powerful Sonnet 29, 'When, in disgrace with Fortune and men's eyes, | I all alone beweep my outcast state,' on the manuscript of her final completed novel *Daniel Deronda* (1875–1876), dedicated to the man she lived with since the mid-1850s, George Henry Lewes (1819–1878). The poem speaks of social isolation and a state of personal self-pity, of the need for assurance. It speaks of a non-comprehending, unsympathetic god: 'And trouble deaf heaven with my bootless cries, | And look upon myself and curse my fate'. The sonnet speaks of total personal lack of confidence and personal jealousy, of 'Wishing me like to one more rich in hope, | Featur'd like him, like him with friends possess'd'. Yet in the final couplet, the final turn of the Sonnet, all is redeemed through personal love: 'For thy sweet love rememb'red such wealth brings | That then I scorn to change my state with kings.'

There are several sonnets that appear different structurally or in other ways from the others. Sonnet 145, beginning 'Those lips that Love's own hand did make', is not in iambic pentameter, unlike most of the others, but consists of eight-syllable (iambic tetrameter) lines. The next sonnet in the sequence, 146, with its opening line, 'Poor soul, the centre of my sinful earth', appears to be more Christian in its sentiments and preoccupied with the saving of the soul, rather than with the body and the obsession with time and mortality that pervades the other sonnets. The final two (153 and 154) focus upon Cupid and seem to draw upon fifth century Greek epigrams. Sonnet 153 opens, 'Cupid laid by his brand [firebrand or flaming torch] and fell asleep; | A maid of Dian's [Diana, the goddess of chastity] this advantage found.'

Sex, desire and lust, dominate many of the sonnets. Sonnet 129, 'Th' expense of spirit in a waste of shame', for instance, is a fine illustration of the play of puns, lexical complications and psychological contradictions in the Sonnets, expressed at times in legal, hunting and fishing metaphors. In the first of the four divisions of the poem, lust is shown as the 'expenditure of vital power (mind and semen) in a wasting of shame (chastity and genitalia), and until action' (Jakobson and Jones: 14), 'lust | is perjur'd, murd'rous, bloody, full of blame, | Savage, extreme, rude [harsh], cruel, not to trust.' In the second division of the sonnet, lust is 'Past reason hunted, and no sooner had, | Past reason hated, as a swallowed bait'. This 'bait' has been 'On purpose laid to make the taker mad'. So, in the third quatrain, that which has been so madly pursued and as soon as had, regretted, is 'A bliss in proof and prov'd, [a] very woe' – a wonderfully contradictory line playing upon the language of 'proof' and 'proved' of a will or contract and the very human emotions of 'bliss' and 'woe'. In the final couplet, again there is a paradox. Human beings know all this, are aware of them but still lust: 'All this the world well knows, yet none knows well | To shun the heaven that leads men to this hell.'

There are various contenders for the young man and the Dark Lady with whom the poet seems obsessed. The young man has been identified with the Earl of Southampton. The other leading male contender, given the dedication in the 1609 Quarto to 'The Onlie Begetter of These . . . Sonnets. Mr. W.H.', is William Herbert (1580–1630), Third Earl of Pembroke. Certainly a patron of Shakespeare's and with his younger brother Philip (1584–1650, the 4th Earl) a co-dedicatee of the *First Folio*. Pembroke, the elder, was a patron to among other dramatists Ben Jonson, Philip Massinger (1583–1640), and Inigo Jones (1573–1652), the architect and designer of court masques. In 1601, he was briefly thrown into prison following an affair with Mary Fitton, one of Queen Elizabeth I's maids of honour, whom he had made pregnant. In common with the Earl of Southampton, he, too, became connected with the Virginia Company.

A. L. Rowse (1903–1997), a leading if somewhat idiosyncratic and controversial English scholar, conjectures in, for instance, *Discovering Shakespeare* (1989) that Emilia Lanier[1] is without question the Dark Lady of the sonnets although there are other candidates too. Probably of Sephardic Jewish origin, the daughter of a court musician, at the age of 20 she became mistress of the Lord Chamberlain and patron of Shakespeare's theatrical company, Henry Carey, the First Lord Hunsdon. In 1593, following her marriage to another court musician, she gave birth to Carey's son. She also consulted in 1597 the influential astrologer and physician Simon Forman (1552–1611), whose notes form the earliest extant descriptions of performances of *Macbeth*, *The Winter's Tale* and *Cymbeline*. Lanier became the first Englishwoman to have published a substantial volume of her own poems with the appearance in 1611 of her *Salve Deus Rex Judaeorum* (Hail, God, King of the Jews). Rowse introduced in 1978 an edition of this under the title *The Poems of Shakespeare's Dark Lady*.

The Phoenix and Turtle

Venus and Adonis, *The Rape of Lucrece* and the Sonnets, profound meditations on mutability, are not Shakespeare's only poems dealing with the mutability theme. Mention should be made of the very powerful and enigmatic lyrical poem of 67 lines, *The Phoenix and Turtle*. It has three sections and is written in trochaic tetrameter metre. The poem originally appeared in *Love's Martyr, or Rosalin's Complaint* (1601), compiled by a Robert Chester (fl. 1601), who worked for Sir John Salusbury of Denbighshire in Wales. Included is a lengthy poem by Chester announced on the title page of the volume as 'Allegorically Shadowing the truth of Love, in the constant Fate of the Phoenix and Turtle.' It has been argued that his poem was written as early as 1586 to celebrate Salusbury's marriage to Ursula Stanley. She was the sister of Lord Strange, the Earl of Derby (d. 1594), whose company (the Strange's Men) were led by Edward Alleyn.

Whether Shakespeare's beautiful and complex allegorical poem was written as early as 1586 is speculation. The poem praises ideal human union through using a tale of the two birds, the legendary Phoenix and the turtledove. Both may be found in the *Song of Songs* (2. 12) and the 'voice of the turtle' as the harbinger of the return of spring reverberates through the Hebrew liturgy. The turtle dove is associated with fertility, with procreation, and the mythical Phoenix with resurrection. In the poem, the latter, the Phoenix, is female and the turtle dove the male.

The style of the poem is most interesting. The lines are short and the poem has a threefold division. First of all, there is a 'Proem', a meeting of the birds, the swan is the priest, and they celebrate the funeral rites of the Phoenix and the turtle dove. They have 'fled | In a mutual flame from hence.' In the seventh stanza, an anthem is sung by the birds:

> So they loved as love in twain
> Had the essence but in one,
> Two distincts, division none:
> Number there in love was slain.

They loved so completely: 'Either was the other's mine.'

The final section is a threnos, or a mourning song, not in lines of four but of three in five stanzas. They are ironically

> Leaving no posterity
> 'Twas not their infirmity,
> It was married chastity.

The Phoenix of myth, known for its regenerative qualities, reproduces no more; it rests eternally. The final stanza is noteworthy for its cumulative, moving and extremely effective monosyllables:

> To this urn let those repair [go]
> That are either true or fair;
> For these dead birds sigh a prayer.

Shakespeare once again plays on meanings of 'fair', with its legal and physical implications and the legal and literal meanings of 'true': not only is the weight or measure of something correct, but there, too, is fidelity, loyalty.[2]

Chapter Four
Working Dramatist: The Comedies

Francis Meres in September 1598 noted among Shakespeare's 'Comedies' *The Two Gentlemen of Verona* (1589–1591), *The Comedy of Errors* (1594), *Love's Labour's Lost* (1594–1595), *A Midsummer Night's Dream* (1595) and the lost *Love's Labour's Won* (1595–1596). Other plays under the category of 'Comedies' included in the *First Folio* and belonging to the last decade of the sixteenth century and the very early years of the following century include *As You Like It* (1599–1600), *The Merchant of Venice* (1598), *Much Ado About Nothing* (1598–1599), *The Taming of the Shrew* (1590–1591) and *Twelfth Night, or What You Will* (1601). The dates within parentheses represent the current dating consensus.

Biographically, these years witness the death in August 1596 of Shakespeare's only son, Hamnet. In 1596, John Shakespeare was granted a coat of arms that he had vainly requested thirty years previously. His son William's status, prosperity and success, is revealed by his May 1596 purchase of New Place, the second-largest house in Stratford. In London in the mid-1590s, Shakespeare lived in the Bishopsgate area, not far from where his company performed. Following the 1599 purchase of the Globe, he dwelt on the South Bank of the Thames River, and in 1604, he had lodgings with the Mountjoys, a French family, in Silver Street, situated near St. Olave's Church. Two years earlier, Shakespeare paid the large amount of £320 for 107 acres of land in the Old Town of Stratford.

The Comedy of Errors

Among the 'Comedies', a Quarto of *Love's Labour's Lost* was published in 1599. A year earlier, *The Merchant of Venice* was entered in

the Stationers' Register on 22 July 1598. Internal evidence and external accounts such as those of eye witnesses reveal much. The probably
earlier *The Two Gentlemen of Verona* is the first of the six 'Comedies'
Meres mentions in his 1598 account, although its first publication
seems to have been in the 1623 *First Folio*. An eye witness records
that on the night of 28 December 1594 at Gray's Inn, London, a
performance of *The Comedy of Errors* created such an uproar that it
had to be curtailed.

> It was thought good not to offer any thing of Account saving
> Dancing and Revelling with Gentlewomen; and after such Sports a
> Comedy of Errors (like to Plautus his *Menechmus*) was played by the
> Players. So that Night was begun, and continued to the end, in noth-
> ing but Confusion and Errors; whereupon it was ever afterwards
> called, *The Night of Errors* (*Riverside*: 1963).

Plautus' (*c*.254–184BC) Roman short comedy, in common with
Shakespeare's comedy, depends for its plot upon mistaken identities,
comic confusion, a long-lost twin brother and romantic interludes.

The Taming of the Shrew

An anonymous *Taming of the Shrew*, much shorter than the play with
the definite article published in the *First Folio* of 1623, appeared in
1594. However, passages from Shakespeare's play are extant from
around as early as 1592, being referred to in an anonymous comedy
A Knack to Know a Knave. A year later, Anthony Chute (d. 1594/5),
includes in his poem *Beauty Dishonoured* the line 'he calls his Kate,
and she must come and kiss him.' The plot of Shakespeare's play has
three elements. In its Induction, a drunken tinker named Christopher
Sly is tricked into believing that he has been transformed into a
Lord for whose entertainment a drama is to be enacted. There then
follows the main plot performed for Sly. In this, the feisty Katherina
is courted, won and apparently controlled, by the fortune hunter
Petruchio. In the third element, Bianca, Katherina's sister, has three
suitors, Lucentio, Gremio and Hortensio. Sexual rivalry, identity,

persuasion, verbal fireworks, and female assertiveness are but some of the key features of one of Shakespeare's most frequently revived 'Comedies'. With the exception of *The Merry Wives of Windsor,* it is the only instance of a Shakespearean comedy set at home in England as opposed to an imaginary or foreign setting.

A Midsummer Night's Dream

Also listed in 1598 by Francis Meres is *A Midsummer Night's Dream.* First printed as a Quarto in 1600 and entered in the Stationers' Register in October 1600, the title page indicates that the play has been 'sundry times publickely acted' by the Lord Chamberlain's Men. Internal references suggest a date even earlier than 1598. Titania tells Oberon of 'Contagious fogs; which, falling in the land, | Hath every pelting river made so proud | That they have overborne their continents' (2. 1. 90–92). Her speech with its reference to inclement weather conditions probably refers to the mid-1594 and late 1596 period during which the English weather behaved unpredictably and there were disastrous harvests. *A Midsummer Night's Dream* in common with *Love's Labour's Lost* is noted for its tremendous variations in poetic styles, use of metre and rhyme schemes. In common with *The Taming of the Shrew*, it, too, contains a play within a play.

A Midsummer Night's Dream witnesses three marriages, dwells upon performance, acting, illusion, all in the setting of an aristocratic wedding set in a luxurious country manor. There are fairies, mythological creations, Queens and Dukes, seemingly incompetent rustics and superb lyrical poetry. This ranges from Lysander's 'The course of true love never did run smooth' (1. 1. 134) to, for instance, the prose poetry of Bottom's: 'The eye of man hath not heard, the ear of man hath not seen, man's hand is not able to taste, his tongue to conceive, nor his heart to report, what my dream was' (4. 1. 211–214). This in itself is a burlesque of lines from 1 Cor. 2. 9–10: '[The] Eye hath not seen, nor ear heard, neither have entered into the heart of man, the things which God hath prepared for them that love him' ['King James' version].

Much Ado About Nothing

Much Ado About Nothing continues the gender debates found in *The Taming of the Shrew, A Midsummer Night's Dream* and *Love's Labour's Lost*. Replete with verbal fireworks, puns and colloquial language, it is not mentioned by Meres in 1598. A Quarto edition was published in 1600 and refers to Will Kempe (d. 1603), the chief comic actor of the period, as Dogberry, the Constable in charge of the Watch. Kempe's name is also found in the 1599 Quarto of *Romeo and Juliet*. However, just following the construction of the Globe in that year, Kempe sold his share and left the King's Men. Robert Armin (*c*.1568–1615) replaced him as the chief comic actor. So *Much Ado About Nothing* probably was performed prior to Kempe's leaving Shakespeare's company. It is entered in the Stationers' Registry for 4 August 1600. Other entries include *As You Like It, Henry V,* and Ben Jonson's *Every Man in His Humour*. The Quarto title page states that *Much Ado About Nothing* 'have been sundrie times publikely acted by the right honourable, the Lord Chamberlaine his seruants'.

An unusual feature of *Much Ado About Nothing* is the extent of its prose usage: just over 70 per cent of the lines in the play being in prose. The other Shakespeare play having as much prose usage is *The Merry Wives of Windsor*, entered in the Stationers' Register in January 1602 and published later in the same year as a Quarto and regarded as a sequel to the *Henry IV* plays (1596–1598). *The Merry Wives of Windsor* has 86.6 per cent of its text in prose. Not withstanding this variant from the pattern of the other comedies, set in Messina, in common with for instance *The Taming of the Shrew*, the plot of *Much Ado About Nothing* has three elements. In the first, Don Pedro, Prince of Arragon, reconciles with his half-brother, the illegitimate Don John, whom he has defeated in battle. As allies, they return to Messina, the capital, as guests of Leonato the Governor. A young nobleman serving Don Pedro, Count Claudio, falls in love with Leonato's daughter, Hero. Don Pedro woos her on Claudio's behalf.

In the second and central plot strand, mainly written in verse, Don John deceives Claudio by making him believe that on the eve of her marriage, Hero has taken a lover. Consequently, Claudio publicly, at the altar, scorns her. There is also a parallel plot, largely in prose, in which Beatrice, Hero's cousin, and Benedick, a friend of both Don Pedro and Claudio, are manipulated through various tricks into self-recognition and then to the realization that they love one another. The third element of the drama is supplied by the lower life characters, clearly English rather than Italian, Constable Dogberry, Verges his assistant and the Watchmen. It is Beatrice and Benedick who have caught the imagination of theatre-goers, readers, and composers such as Hector Berlioz (1803–1869), whose two-act comic opera *Béatrice et Bénédict*, with its magnificent overture, is based upon *Much Ado About Nothing*.

As You Like It

Also not mentioned by Meres is *As You Like It*, recorded in the Stationers' Register on 4 August 1600. This drama uses pastoral conventions emphasizing country as well as court settings and characters. The setting is largely in the woods; there is a good deal of artifice, songs, poems and a very romantic conclusion. Much prose is used and there are five songs. 'It was a lover and his lass, | With a hey, and a ho, and a hey | nonino,' sung in Act 5, Scene 3, was set to music with lute accompaniment and is found in Thomas Morley's (*c*.1557–1602) *First Book of Ayres* (1600). It is among the few songs in Shakespeare for which the contemporary music is extant.

There are considerable stylistic and other parallels, especially in the plot between *As You Like It* and *Rosalynde*, a prose romance written in 1586–1587 and published in 1590 by Thomas Lodge (1557/8–1625), which by 1598 had gone into a fourth edition. This uses the pastoral mode and contains rival dukes. Shakespeare transposes them into brothers and the usurper repents so that the exiled court is able to be restored, whereas in Lodge there is a bloody battle during which the usurper is killed. Further, Shakespeare changes most of the names. Both Lodge and Shakespeare focus upon the emerging love between a disguised Rosalind, who has dressed as a boy, Ganymede, and Orlando, a younger brother cruelly treated by his elder brother, Oliver. The latter becomes transformed by the love of Rosalind's cousin, Celia. Hymen, the god of marriage, is introduced by Shakespeare to resolve the problems and entanglements. Shakespeare also creates the jester, Touchstone, and Jaques, a melancholy courtier. These two, although representing differing perspectives, act as commentators upon the action.

Characteristics of Shakespearean Comedy

Shakespeare's Comedies have certain characteristics.

- They are not necessarily funny; indeed there is much melancholia and sadness in them, but they don't end in death, as Shakespeare's Tragedies do.
- They each contain ultimate resolutions represented in a gender pairing off. For instance, Rosalind with Orlando and Celia with Oliver in *As You Like It*.
- They involve deception, especially in gender terms, with, for instance, young women dressing as young boys.
- They contain at times complicated interlocking plots with the sub-plots assisting in the revelation of the main plot. Beatrice and Benedick, for example, in *Much Ado About Nothing*, belong to the sub-plot rather than the main plot, which focuses on Don John's deception of Claudio.
- They contain a 'love story', ideas of 'love', or perceptions of 'love'.
- There is much interaction between 'high', or aristocratic social elements and characters, and low-born characters and rustic elements. In other words, the high-born mix with the low-born.
- In some, but not all of the Comedies, there is a foil, a malcontent refusing to participate in the general revels or happiness of the others. The melancholy Jaques in *As You Like It* is one example. More serious ones representing differing sets of values than the hedonistic, fun-loving values of many of the characters are represented in the figures of Shylock and Malvolio. They add a differing social and moral dimension to the drama.
- Music plays a central role in many of the Comedies. In *Twelfth Night*, the Fool becomes the commentator upon the action and serves in modern terms as a counsellor or therapist to the Duke his master.

- Some of the action of the Comedies takes place across the sea in islands, or in a forest, as for example in *A Midsummer Night's Dream* or *As You Like It*.
- These plays are largely set outside of England. *As You Like It,* for instance, in the Ardenne region of France, although there also was a Forest of Ardenne in Shakespeare's Warwickshire.
- Most are replete with word and phrase repartee, with hyperbole or exaggeration, although these devices are by no means confined to the Comedies. In *Twelfth Night,* for instance, Viola, still disguised as a Page, Cesario, 'A thousand deaths would die' if he/she is still separated from the Duke (5. 1. 133).

Many of the Comedies, especially in the actions of the low-life characters, depict misrule, carnival and anarchy. This is best represented in the figure of Sir Toby Belch, who as his name suggests, has transcended good manners – he belches-and knows no restraint (apart of course, ironically, from the physical restraints imposed by his usually drunken state).

Two plays, classified in the *First Folio* as 'Comedies', do, however, stretch the limits of the term. They have many of the characteristics of the genre but contain an underlying sadness bordering on tragedy.

The Merchant of Venice

The Stationers' Register for 22 July 1598 contains the entry of 'a book of *The Merchant of Venice* or Otherwise Called *The Jew of Venice*'. The Quarto version of 1600 was titled 'The Most Excellent History of the Merchant of Venice. With the Extreme Cruelty of Shylock the Jew toward the Said Merchant, in Cutting a Just Pound of his Flesh: and the Obtaining of Portia by the Choice of Three Chests.'

Such a title passes judgement on Shylock as the villain of the play. Christopher Marlowe's *The Jew of Malta* (*c.*1589) focuses upon Barabas, whose daughter Abigail falls in love with a Christian. Following Barabas's killing of her suitor, she becomes a nun. Shylock's daughter

Jessica, however, betrays her father, steals from him and elopes with Lorenzo. At the opening of the final act of the play, they are given some of the most beautiful lyrical poetry tinged with irony, cruelty and prejudice. Lorenzo observes: 'The moon shines bright. In such a night as this | When the sweet wind did gently kiss the trees,' and adds:

> In such a night
> Did Jessica steal from the wealthy Jew,
> And with an unthrift love did run from Venice,
> As far as Belmont.

He describes to her the music of the spheres:

> How sweet the moonlight sleeps upon this bank!
> Here will we sit, and let the sounds of music
> Creep in our ears. Soft stillness and the night
> Become the touches of sweet harmony (5. 1–2, 14–16, 54–57).

Assonance, alliteration, run-on lines, musical metaphors and the expression of romantic love, are subsequently counterpointed in the act by punning on the significance of a ring and to whom it was presented. Disguise, role-playing, a world to escape to – in this instance, Belmont, across the water from the realities of Venice – are features common to Shakespeare's other Comedies. What is not common is the intensity of vision, the depiction of centuries of hatred and persecution levelled at Shylock, who demands his bond, his payment in the exact amount of a pound of flesh after he has agreed to loan his enemy Antonio, who has continually taunted him, 3,000 ducats for three months. Shylock insists upon strict repayment following the running aground of Antonio's ship and the inability to repay.

Tricked by a brilliant lawyer, Portia disguised, Shylock is humiliated in the great trial scene. Previously, Solario and Solanio try to persuade Shylock not to take Antonio's flesh, as Solario says, 'What's that good for?' Shylock delivers in prose one of the great speeches in Shakespeare. He tells Solario and Solanio:

> Hath not a Jew eyes? Hath not a Jew hands, organs, dimensions [physical form], senses, affections, passions; fed with the same food,

hurt with the same weapons, subject to the same diseases, heal'd by the same means, warm'd and cool'd by the same winter and summer, as a Christian is? If you prick us, do we not bleed? If you tickle us, do we not laugh? If you poison us, do we not die? And if you wrong us, shall we not revenge? If we are like you in the rest, we will resemble you in that. (3. 1. 52, 59–68)

Shylock's goods, his property, are confiscated. He is forced to convert. His final words in the play are the ironic 'I am content' and 'I am not well. Send the deed after me, | And I will sign it' (4. 1. 394, 396–397). Even the ring his wife, Leah, gave him is stolen by his daughter. Shylock comments using a fantastic, surrealistic image: 'I would not have given it for a wilderness of monkeys' (3. 1. 122).

The great Jewish German poet and critic Heinrich Heine (1797–1856) saw the great actor Edmund Kean (1787/9–1833) perform Shylock on 26 January 1814 at Drury Lane. Heine comments, 'I must place *The Merchant of Venice* among Shakespeare's tragedies although he intended it as a comedy surrounding it by merry masks, satyrs and cupids' (*Baker, Vickers, Shakespeare: The Critical Tradition*, 54). It isn't a tragedy. Antonio's fortunes are restored to him. Portia, no longer in disguise, gains Bassanio, the man she loves, when he chooses the right casket. The other suitors have made the wrong choices; they, like Antonio, have risked all and gained nothing. The drama concludes with Gratiano's crude, sexually suggestive pun: 'Well, while I live I'll fear no other thing | So sore, as keeping safe Nerissa's ring' (5. 1. 306–307). Shylock, one can only assume, is left alone to sign the document if he doesn't have a stroke before doing so.

There are internal allusions in the play that assist in its dating, allocating it to the late 1590s. It is unlikely that it could have been written before 1596, as in the opening act there is a reference to 'my wealthy *Andrew* [dock'd] in sand, | Vailing her high top lower than her ribs | To kiss her burial' (1. 1. 27–28). Andrew was the name of the Spanish ship *St. Andrew* captured in a summer 1596 English naval raid on Cadiz. It is also probable that Shakespeare's play draws upon Christopher Marlowe's *The Jew of Malta,* performed by the Admiral's Men in 1594. Henslowe's diary reveals that 'plays entitled *The Jew* and *The Jew of Malta* . . . formed the subject of no less than twenty representations between May 1594 and the end of the year' (Baker and Vickers: 139). The reason for its popularity had to do with the 1594 trial and execution of Roderigo Lopez (*c*.1517–1594), the Queen's physician, a Portuguese Jew, accused of attempting to poison Elizabeth. One of the leading London medical authorities, he was known to the Earl of Leicester, Burghley and Essex. Lopez (Lupus meaning wolf in Latin) was accused of being an agent of King Philip of Spain. In Act 4, Scene 1 of *The Merchant of Venice* Gratiano refers to 'a wolf, who hang'd for human slaughter' (4. 1. 134) – a punning allusion to Lopez.

Twelfth Night, or What You Will

Like Shylock, Malvolio in *Twelfth Night* is also out of place, condemned to be omitted from the comic circle. He, too, strikes a tragic note in the comic vision turning sour. *Twelfth Night, or What You Will* is the only Shakespearean play whose title offers an alternative. 'Twelfth Night' refers specifically to the Feast of the Epiphany or the twelfth night after Christmas day and the culmination of the Christmas festivities. It was a major celebration in Elizabethan times, a day for revels, entertainments in one form or another. Epiphany represented a very important Christian festival, commemorating the coming of the Magi to Bethlehem bearing gifts, Jesus of Nazareth's baptism and the miracle of Cana when water was turned into wine (see Jn 2. 3–11). By Shakespeare's time it had become a riot, a saturnalia, the Feast of Fools, especially wildly celebrated in the elite Inns of Court, where lawyers trained, and the Universities. In other words, 'Twelfth Night' was associated with an overturning of the routines of order and customs. This is exactly the pattern of the play.

The other title 'What You Will' is interesting. 'Will' possessed for Elizabethans the sense it has today of a wish, an inclination. There was also the meaning of irrational desire and passion – frequently physical – uncontrolled by judgement, or in other words, a loss of control. Of course, 'Will' is also bawdy, referring to the male sexual organ. This alternative title invites audiences or readers to react as they wish to the play. Charles I (1600–1649) marked his copy of the Second Folio (1632) with the name of the Puritan spoiler of the play, 'Malvolio', who opposed Sir Toby Belch's hedonism (*Riverside*: [437]).

Twelfth Night, or What You Will saw its initial printing in the *First Folio* of 1623, there being no Quarto edition, and it was registered in the Stationers' Register on 8 November 1623. There is a much earlier witness to the play's performance in the notebook of a law student at the Middle Temple, John Manningham (d. 1622). He records on 2 February 1602 seeing a performance in the Middle Temple Hall: 'At our feast wee had a play called "Twelue Night, or What You Will" much like the Commedy of Errores or Menechmi in Plautus.' Manningham then observes,

> a good practise in it to make the Steward [Malvolio] beleeve his Lady widdowe [Olivia] was in love with him, by counterfeyting a letter as from his Lady in generall termes, telling him what shee liked best in him, and prescribing his gesture in smiling, his apparaile &c.

Manningham's diary note concludes 'and then when he came to practise making him beleeue they took him to be mad' (cited Chambers: II: 327–328).

There are internal allusions suggesting that the play was written prior to 1602. Maria refers to 'the new map, with the augmentation of the Indies' (3.2. 79–80). This map first appeared in Richard Hakluyt (?1552–1616), the travel writer and geographer's *The Principal Navigations, Voyages and Discoveries of the English Nation,* 1599 edition. The song 'Farewell, dear heart' (2. 3. 102), appeared in Robert Jones's (fl. 1597–1615) the composer's *First Book of Songs and Airs* (1600). Also, Feste's opinion that the phrase 'out of my welkin-I might say of my "element"' is 'overworn' (3. 1. 59) is an allusion to Thomas Dekker's *Satiromastix,* first performed by Shakespeare's theatrical company in 1601.

Manningham's is an excellent account of one portion of the plot of a play, that in common with so many of Shakespeare's other comedies, depends upon disguise and deception. Orsino, Duke of Illyria, believes he is in love. The play opens with his lines addressed to the accompanying musicians, 'If music be the food of love, play on', the emphasis being on the first word 'If.' Of course, the Duke's state of mind might well represent an enormous illusion: he may well not be in love at all. The doubts initially are implied by the sense that the

Duke needs sustenance; he needs 'food' represented by music to sustain 'love' (1. 1. 1).

Viola is alone with a captain and sailors after being shipwrecked on an unknown island. She has to adapt to survive in her new surroundings. After discovering that her new world is that 'of a noble duke, in nature as in name' named Orsino, she disguises herself: 'I'll serve this duke; | Thou shalt present me as an eunuch to him' (1. 2. 25, 55–56). She changes gender, her costume, her gestures and her voice to become a young man, Cesario. She is so convincing in her role, in her new sexual identity (or non-sexual as she is a 'eunuch'), that the duke becomes infatuated with 'her' and falls in love with 'her'.

The illusion, the deception, is made even more ironic if it is remembered that, incredibly, apparently women did not perform on the English stage, certainly on the London stage, although they may have done so in the country, until the Restoration of the monarchy in 1660. All women's parts, the roles apparently were performed by boys dressed as women, or by castrati, those whose sexual organs were removed in order that their voices would remain high. Illusion, disguise, confusion in sexual gender are common to Shakespeare's comedies. Also common are tricks, often cruel ones such as that played upon Malvolio, whose vanity and ambition to rise up the social ladder persuade him to accept the veracity of the scheming Maria. She serves Olivia and succeeds in rising up the social ladder by marrying the drunken joker, but a well-connected aristocratic one, Sir Toby Belch. Malvolio, blinded by his own ambition, is narcissistic. Olivia tells him: 'O, you are sick of self-love, Malvolio, and taste with a distemper'd appetite' (1. 5. 91). He is all too ready to believe the forged letter Maria leaves in his way, which indicates that, to gain his mistress Olivia's affections, he should dress up in ridiculous clothing: 'I will be strange, stout, in yellow stockings, and cross-garter'd, even with the swiftness of putting on' (2. 5. 169–172).

Presumed mad, to have lost his reason, he is locked up in darkness and further tricked, this time by the clown Feste pretending to be Sir Topas, a curate who has been sent to ascertain whether Malvolio is crazy. Sir Topas gives him light, ink and paper so that he may address the assumed beloved Olivia. In the final scene of the play, Malvolio addresses Olivia in powerful, moving words: 'Madam, you have done me wrong, | Notorious wrong.' The truth is revealed and

Olivia tells him, 'Alas, poor fool, how have they baffled thee!' Malvolio, like Shylock, is not part of the revels; he is banished. His final words are more appropriate to the world of the Tragedies than to the comic universe: 'I'll be reveng'd on the whole pack of you!' To this, Olivia can only respond, 'He hath been most notoriously abus'd.' But this is not a tragedy. In the spirit of Shakespearean comedy, nobody dies or is murdered, and revenge is not fully enacted (at least not within the play). The duke instructs the servants to: 'Pursue him, and entreat him to a peace' (5. 1. 327–328, 369, 378–380).

Maria's trick is motivated by revenge. Malvolio has tried to impose order and restraint upon the unruly, the uncontrollable. Sir Toby, with Sir Andrew Aguecheek, his companion whose last name implies ague, leanness and disease, and indeed possible sexual disease, are behaving late at night exceedingly boisterously with the Clown. They are so drunk that even Maria protests: 'What a caterwauling do you keep here!' In other words, they are sounding and behaving like cats. Predictably, Malvolio, the steward, interrupts the revels: 'My masters, are you mad? Or what are you? Have you no wit, manners nor honesty, but to gabble like tinkers at this time of night? Do ye make an ale-house of my lady's house?' They are accused of madness; ironically, by the end of the play, the revellers have transformed the keeper of order and decorum into one accused of madness.

Sir Toby's reply to Malvolio represents a fundamental clash of values reflecting a clash increasingly prevalent in the early seventeenth century. He tells Malvolio that socially he has exceeded his place, his rank: 'Art any more than a steward?' or a servant. Furthermore, 'Dost thou think because thou art virtuous there shall be no more cakes and ale?' Maria then describes Malvolio: 'sometimes he is a kind of puritan.' The differences in values are stark and significant. Sir Toby's are those of hedonism and pleasure. 'Cakes and ale' are by tradition associated with festive occasions. Puritans do not drink or indulge in excess. The distinctions are to take on serious ramifications. A decade or so after the initial performance of *Twelfth Night*, the Pilgrim Fathers sailed from Plymouth to the New World. In the 1640s, the English Civil War saw a clash between the various forces of Puritanism and the Royalists, or Cavaliers. During the Interregnum and the Republic (*c*.1650–*c*.1659), there was a premium placed on festivities and drinking, and the theatres, perceived as immoral, were largely closed. So Sir Toby's rhetorical interrogative response to Malvolio 'out of tune sir! ye lie' (2. 3. 72, 86–89, 114–116, 113) refers on one level to a lack of a singing and dancing facility. It is also prophetic, as Sir Toby, the hedonist from the Puritan's perspective, has indeed outlived his day.

In common with other Shakespearean drama, not only his Comedies, this play is replete with sexual innuendos and puns. Rings are lost and found. Malvolio, when he breaks the wax seal of the forged letter that he assumes to be from his mistress Olivia, finds 'Her c's her u's and her t's'(2. 5. 89), not her 'n's'. There, too, are identical twins in the drama. Sebastian, assumed lost at sea, is the twin brother of Viola, who is disguised as Cesario. Music and song too play a prominent part. Its chief exponent is Feste, the Clown, Olivia's jester. Viola praises him in paradoxical terms: 'This fellow is wise enough to play the fool, | And to do that well craves a kind of wit.' The final word 'wit' (3. 1. 60–61) here having the sense of high intelligence. There is also a wise fool in *As You Like It*. Such a character is not confined to the comedies and is found, too, in *King Lear*.

As the jester in the great tragedy *King Lear*, Feste, the wise fool, acts in the capacity of a counsellor or a therapist. In the instance of *Twelfth Night*, he advises Olivia, the countess, and the Duke. He counsels her that it is unwise to lament forever on a loss that cannot be brought back. He sings 'In delay there lies no plenty, | Then come kiss me, sweet and twenty | Youth's a stuff will not endure' (2. 3. 50–52). Feste is all too aware of the fragility and transience of life. As all great Shakespearean drama, *Twelfth Night* is pervaded with a sense of sadness and mutability. One of its chief spokespersons is Feste. At the end of the drama, his is the concluding summation in a song encompassing the stages of life from 'a little tine boy' to old age. Feste's wisdom is that 'the rain it raineth every day' and that 'A great while ago the world begun.' His final words are 'But that's all one, our play is done. | And we'll strive to please you every day' (5. 1. 389, 392, 405, 407–408). Although there is an inevitability of existence, the dramatist, and his players aim 'to please' (408) and to satisfy their audience. In the world of the Shakespearean comedy, none of the characters die within the play. That is not the case in either the histories and especially the tragedies, in which revenge must inevitably have its day.

Chapter Five
Political Unrest: Elizabeth's Last Years

Biographical Recapitulation

Concerning Shakespeare's life during the last two decades of the sixteenth century, the following can be firmly asserted. On 28 November 1582, a marriage license bond was issued in Worcester for 'Willim Shagspere' and 'Anne Hathwey'. The baptism of 'Susanna daughter to William Shakspere' was witnessed in Stratford ' 26 May 1583, and 2 February 1585 saw the baptism of 'Hamnet & Judeth sonne & daughter to Willia[m] Shakspere'. In 1589, William Shakespeare is referred to in a lawsuit bought by his parents against a John Lambert relating to property near Stratford at Wilmcot. There are additions to Robert Greene's 1592 affirmation of Shakespeare as a writer who was already making waves in the London literary firmament. In 1594 and 1595, there are references to Shakespeare's authorship of *The Rape of Lucrece*. On 15 March 1595, Shakespeare's name appears as a joint payee of the Lord Chamberlain's Men for court performances, again demonstrating that Shakespeare was very much a force to be reckoned with on the London theatrical scene. As noted, in 1593, a first Quarto of *Venus and Adonis* was published. Henslowe's diary records that a play with the title 'titus & ondrinicus' was performed at the Rose Theatre on 24 January 1594. On 3 March 1592, Henslowe recorded a 'new' performance of 'Harry the VI' in his diary.

Stratford Archives record the burial of 'Hamnet filius William Shakspere' in Stratford-upon-Avon on 11 August 1596. In October of the same year, Shakespeare's father is associated with two draft grants of arms. On 4 May 1597, and subsequently, there are extant documents recording William Shakespeare's acquisition of the prestigious New Place in the town. However, on 15 November of the same year, a 'William Shackspere' of Bishopsgate, London, occurs in the lists of those not paying taxes due in February 1597. In 1598, Shakespeare's actual name appears on the title page of the second Quartos of *Richard II* and *Richard III*: the first Quarto of the former appeared in 1597 and the latter a year later. *Richard III* was entered in the Stationers' Register on 20 October 1598. Shakespeare's name also appears in a 1598 Quarto of *Love's Labour's Lost* claiming to be 'Newly corrected and augmented'.

In 1598, Francis Meres in his *Palladis Tamia* lists six Shakespearean 'Comedies' and six 'Tragedies', of which only *Titus Andronicus* and *Romeo and Juliet* are designated as 'Tragedies' in the *First Folio*, the remainder being 'Histories'. In the last two years of the century, extant references to William Shakespeare become much more extensive than previously. Once again, he is listed as a tax defaulter in Bishopsgate, on 1 October 1598. On 15 October 1598, Richard Quiney, a local Stratford dignitary, requests a £30 loan from Shakespeare. An inventory records on 16 May 1599 that the newly constructed Globe theatre is occupied by 'William Shakespeare and others'. On 6 October 1599 and 6 October 1600, a 'Willmus Shakspere' is named as owing money, this time to the Exchequer in London.

Henry IV, Parts 1 and 2, Henry V

There is no doubt that the 1590s were a tremendously creative and professionally successful period for William Shakespeare. The first part of *Parts 1 and 2 Henry IV* was entered in the Stationers' Register in February 1598 (it is described as 'The History of Henry the IIIIth with his battle of Shrewsbury against Henry Hotspur of the North with the conceited mirth of Sir John Falstaff'); the second part was entered in the Stationers' Register in August 1600. *Henry V* was first printed in Quarto in 1600 and said to have been 'sundry times played by the Right Honourable the Lord Chamberlain his servants'. In other words, it belongs to a pre-1600 dating. Internal evidence suggests as much.

The Chorus is absent from the Quarto but appears in the subsequent 1623 *First Folio* version of the text. In this, in the Chorus's lines opening the fifth act, the Chorus refers to

Were now the general of our gracious Empress,
As in good time he may, from Ireland coming,
Bringing rebellion broached on his sword,
How many would the peaceful city quit
To welcome him! (5. 0. 30–34).

Editors explicate the reference to 'the general' as being to 'Robert Devereux, Earl of Essex, who had left England on 27 March 1599 to suppress Tyrone's rebellion in Ireland. He returned unsuccessful on 28 September'. Following an interview with 'our gracious Empress' shortly after his return, he was placed under house arrest, not being released until 26 August 1600. In January 1601, Essex 'plotted to seize Whitehall'. Following the discovery of the plot, he led an armed uprising against the Queen on 8 February. Londoners did not come to his support; 'he surrendered, was convicted of compassing the Queen's death, and was beheaded on 25 February' 1601 (Craik, ed., Arden edition: 335, 2).

Elizabeth I's Closing Years

The period of Shakespeare's great creative productivity was one of internal transition within the country. The closing years of Elizabeth I's reign and regime were uncertain ones. In 1588, the Spanish Armada, through a combination of bad weather and sheer bad luck, had been smashed on the rocks off the west coast of Ireland and elsewhere. A year earlier, Mary Queen of Scots was executed for treason. The Elizabethan monarchy was still surrounded by internal and external enemies. France, Ireland and the Lowlands were in turmoil; Spain was waiting for revenge; Scotland was unsettled. Its monarch, James VI (1566–1625), Elizabeth's distant cousin who succeeded her in 1603, married Anne of Denmark in 1590. Believing himself to be bewitched by devils during the honeymoon, the marriage was not consummated and savage witch trials took place in Scotland. However, Henry, his first son, was born in 1595; he died from typhoid fever aged 18 in 1612. Another son, Charles, destined to succeed his father as Charles I, was born in 1600. In 1595, Hugh O'Neill, Earl of Tyrone (1540–1616), resisting the increasing annexation of his country Ireland, rebelled. An approximately nine-year war followed, including various attempts at a truce. One was arranged in September 1599 between O'Neill and the Earl of Essex, much to the Queen's displeasure.

Sir Walter Raleigh

Elizabeth was in a very sensitive position. The Anglo-Spanish war and the Irish Rebellion were drawing her resources and energies and that of her counsellors. While she had favourites, Essex being one of them, the Queen had never married and consequently had no heirs. Various efforts had been made to replenish her treasury through overseas ventures. For instance, the writer, soldier and explorer Walter Raleigh (*c.*1554–1618), who earlier served in Ireland in 1580, became a popular courtier but fell out of favour and was thrown into jail in 1592 for marrying a maid of honour to the Queen without appropriate permission. He led an expedition to Guiana on the South American coast in 1595. In Ireland, he met the great poet Edmund Spenser (*c.*1552–1599) who spent most of his life as a colonial civil servant there. The first three books of Spenser's *The Faerie Queene* (1596) were presented to his Queen and the poem celebrates England's cultural and historical past.[3] A few years after Raleigh's expedition, the East India Company was created in order to trade in the East. Indeed, the conflict with Spain was not necessarily only a religious one, England being a Protestant country and Spain a Catholic one, but an economic one, too.

England in the Early 1600s

Troilus and Cressida

The situation in England in the early 1600s was then one of considerable uncertainty. No wonder a character such as Ulysses in the opening act of *Troilus and Cressida* speaks of a real fear of chaos, of 'Each thing [meets] | In mere oppugnancy' or total opposition (1. 3. 110–111). The tragicomedy, one of pointless love played out against the backdrop of a pointless war, is probably the last one Shakespeare wrote prior to Queen Elizabeth's death and was recorded in the Stationers' Register in February 1603. Robert Bridges (1844–1930), a Poet Laureate, largely forgotten today, in lines from his sonnet 'Melancholia,' encapsulates the mood of the years in which Elizabeth I's death was awaited:

> Incertainty that once gave scope to dream
> Of laughing enterprise and glory untold,
> Is now a blackness that no stars redeem,
> A wall of darkness in a night of cold
>
> (cited John Dover Wilson, *The Essential Shakespeare*: 37).

Henry IV, Part 1

This then is the background of what are by general consensus the great History Plays: the two parts of *Henry IV and Henry V. Henry IV, Part I* differs from the other History Plays that are largely based upon Ralph Holinshed's *Chronicles of England, Scotland and Ireland*. The character of Sir John Falstaff and his companions, Prince Harry's (Hal's) associates and the comic elements are new. The Stationers' Register entry of February 1598 succinctly summarizes the two strands of the play: 'The history of Henry the IIIIth with his battle of Shrewsbury against Henry Hotspur of the North with the conceited mirth of Sir John Falstaff.' The title *The First Part of Henry the Fourth*, however, did not appear until the *First Folio* of 1623.

The 1623 text complied with the 1606 'Act to Restrain Abuses of Players'. Ten pound fines were levied for each instance of an actor 'jestingly or profanely' uttering the name of God or Jesus Christ. Consequently, words such as 'zounds' (in other words, 'Gods wounds') were in many instances replaced by 'why' or 'come'. Exclamations such as 'O God!' became 'O heaven!' The earlier Quarto versions of 1598 (two of them), 1599 and 1604 (there were also Quarto versions in 1608, 1613 and 1622) reveal the popularity of the play and are much racier than the post-1606 versions.

Other kinds of censorship were also at work. Initially Falstaff, Peto and Bardolph were named 'Oldcastle', 'Harvey' and 'Russell' respectively.

Sir John Oldcastle (*c*.1378–1417) was regarded as a Protestant martyr, especially by John Foxe (1516–1587), the Protestant theologian who had been exiled during the reign of Mary Tudor. Oldcastle was a follower of John Wyclif (d. 1384), the 'theologian, philosopher and religious reformer' (*ODNB*), and as a Lollard, he was condemned for treason and executed in 1517 by Henry V. This did not stop his descendants, the highly influential Cobham family (William Brooke Cobham, was Lord Chamberlain from August 1596 to March 1597) from objecting to the name. Consequently, in the first Quarto, it was changed to Sir John Falstaff. 'Harvey' became Peto in order to avoid confusion with Sir William Harvey (d. 1642), who was just about to make a very prestigious marriage with the widowed mother of the Earl of Southampton. 'Russell' became Bardolph, as Russell was the surname of the influential Earl of Bedford (*c*.1587–1641) descended from Lord John of Lancaster (1389–1435) commended by Prince Henry following the Battle of Shrewsbury (July 1403: see Dobson and Wells: 188).

Historical memories were still raw. The Battle of Shrewsbury occurs in the play. In this key 1403 battle, Prince Hal defeated the powerful Percy family outside of Shrewsbury, thus ensuring the succession. Henry IV's ascendancy to the throne is depicted in *Richard II*. His sense of guilt for the deposition of what was perceived as the divinely appointed King Richard raises its head in the play. *Henry IV Part 1* oscillates between serious issues regarding the fate of the kingdom, the lives of those involved in the power struggles, and the comic represented by various characters. Henry's son, Hal, bridges the two worlds, that of the court and intrigue in the highest circles, and the taverns and the brothels.

In the first part of the play, Hal is pitted in a fierce power struggle with ruthless political enemies. Glendower, the headstrong Hotspur, Mortimer and Worcester – powerful, influential figures – rebel against Henry IV. At Glendower's castle far away from London in rural Wales, they scheme to divide England into three parts after they have rebelled. However, Wales is also a land of mystery, spirits and temptation. Mortimer doesn't have a stomach to fight, being too much in love with Glendower's daughter. Glendower himself seems entrapped by 'the air a thousand leagues from hence' (3. 1. 224). Hotspur is, in Hal's parodic words, 'he that kills me or some six or seven dozen of Scots at a breakfast, washes his hands, and says to his wife "Fie upon this quiet life! I want work."' Hotspur is consumed with pride and rashness. Hal contemptuously describes another rebel as 'He that rides at high speed with his pistol kills a sparrow flying' (2. 4. 102–105, 344–345).

Hal, on the other hand, is manipulative. For instance, at the conclusion of the initial scene in which he appears, he reveals in a soliloquy his insights into his tavern companions.

> I know you all, and will awhile uphold
> The unyok'd humour of your idleness,
> Yet herein will I imitate the sun,
> Who doth permit the base contagious clouds
> To smother up his beauty from the world,
> That when he please again to be himself,
> Being wanted, he may be more wond'red at
> By breaking through the foul and ugly mists
> Of vapors that did seem to strangle him.

Here is a warning revelation. Hal is play-acting, all is not what it seems; indeed, note 'vapors that did seem to strangle him' – the key word being 'seem' (1. 2. 195–203). Once he has used his drinking companions for his own amusement and education, he will drop them flat. Hal has to bide his time before becoming king. He has to amuse himself and at the same time gain an education in the world he will one day govern as supreme ruler.

The King of the taverns is Oldcastle – Falstaff, who acts as the Prince's surrogate father, educating him in the state of the world, as 'my old lad of the castle' (1. 2. 41–42). He educates his pupil only too well in anarchic behaviour and conduct, in immediate physical gratification, in eating, drinking and jesting. Falstaff, a carnivalesque, Rabelaisian, larger-than-life figure who revels in his huge body, at times takes over the drama. At one point, Falstaff becomes the King and Harry (Hal) his Prince. The Prince protects Falstaff and his companions when the arm of the law comes to arrest them for robbery. In the meantime, an exhausted, overweight Knight Falstaff falls asleep and the young Prince rifles through his pockets, discovering accounts for small amounts of food and enormous amounts of drink.

He settles the unpaid bills and finds for Falstaff and some of his companions positions in his father's army for the upcoming battle with the rebels.

At the conclusion of the play, following Hal's killing of Hotspur, Falstaff appears to be dead, too. After he has left, Falstaff with difficulty raises himself from the ground. He takes credit for the killing, somehow putting Hotspur's body on his back: 'I'll swear I killed him. Why may not he rise as well as I? Nothing confutes me but eyes, and nobody sees me.' He even stabs the dead Hotspur, then swearing to Prince Hal the real slayer: 'I'll take it on my death, I gave him this wound in the thigh. If the man were alive and would deny it, 'zounds, I would make him eat a piece of my sword.' In the words of Prince Hal, 'This is the strangest tale that ever I heard' (5. 4. 125–127, 150–152, 155).

Hal's distancing from Falstaff, his brutal rejection of him, will take place in *Henry IV Part 2*. In the final scene of the first part, father and son are reconciled and order has to be restored in the land. The affairs of state are paramount. The anarchic forces represented by Falstaff on the comic tavern level must be subdued. Yet Falstaff has run away with the critical reception of the play. To use the words of one of the greatest of Shakespearean critics, Dr. Samuel Johnson (1709–1784), also a corpulent character, '*Falstaff*, unimitated, unimitable, *Falstaff*, how shall I extol thee? Thou compound of sense and vice; of sense which may be admired but not esteemed, of vice which may be despised, but hardly detested' (cited Dobson and Wells: 190–191).

The Merry Wives of Windsor

Although Falstaff in *Henry IV Part 2* is dismissed with contempt by his former boon companion with the cruel words, 'I know thee not, old man, fall to thy prayers. | How ill white hairs becomes a fool and jester!' (*Henry IV, Part 2*: 5. 5. 47–48), he refuses to lie down and is resurrected in *The Merry Wives of Windsor*. Tradition holds that the comedy was especially commissioned by Elizabeth I, who wished to see Falstaff in love. Entered in the Stationers' Register in January 1602, the title appeared in a Quarto version in the same year. The Quarto title page reads that the play was performed 'at court . . .

before Her Majestie': no other Shakespearean Quarto claims to have actually been the subject of a royal performance. The comic plot is drawn from multiple sources yet has little to do with English history. It reveals the popularity of Shakespeare's great comic creation depicted in his old age – Falstaff. Musically, the buffoon is also transformed in what is regarded by many discerning voices as Guiseppe Verdi's (1813–1901) greatest opera and incidentally his last, *Falstaff* (1889–1893) written when he was nearly 80. So great was Falstaff's impact not merely on Shakespeare's Queen or Dr Johnson but on the greatest of creative operatic imaginations, Verdi.

Henry IV Part 2

Entered in the Stationers' Register in August 1600, the play appeared also in the same year in a Quarto version. The title page of this draws attention to the dual themes of the play, royal history and the world of Falstaff and his friends, in other words the comic world of the taverns: 'The Second Part of Henrie the fourth Continuing to his death, and coronation of Henrie the fifth. With the humours of Sir John Falstaff, and swaggering Pistol. As it hath been sundry times publically acted by the right honourable, the Lord Chamberlain his servants. Written by William Shakespeare.'

Similar sources as for the first part are drawn upon, including the anonymous play *The Famous Victories of Henry V*, entered in the Stationers' Register in 1594 and published in 1598, and Holinshed and Samuel Daniels' (1562–1619) *Four Books of the Civil Wars* (1595). These are juxtaposed with the comic inventiveness of the non-historical scenes involving Falstaff. The historical scenes are serious in tone. Initially, Prince Hal appears to have returned to his former anarchic behaviour. His father is beset by many problems and has deferred his promised pilgrimage to Jerusalem. Rebellion is again afoot. His father is also extremely concerned about his son. At the conclusion of Act 4, Hal appears at the bed of his dying father. Mistakenly believing him to be dead, he takes the crown and places it on his own head: 'Lo where it sits, | Which God still guard; and put the world's whole strength | Into one giant arm'. In 'the next room,' Hal is 'Washing with with kindly tears his gentle cheeks' (4. 5. 43–45, 82–83).

Falstaff, on the other hand, when he hears that Henry IV is dead and that Hal is now King, cries out 'Let us take any man's horses, the laws of England are at my commandment' (5. 3. 136–137).

Henry is obsessed by his son's irresponsibility, imagining the plight of his country under Hal, who 'from curb'd license plucks | The muzzle of restraint'. As he dies, Henry IV openly acknowledges his past and his crimes in words that are replete with irony in the light of what is to happen to his son:

> God knows, my son,
> By what by-paths and indirect crook'd ways
> I met this crown, and I myself know well
> How troublesome it sate upon my head.
> To thee it shall descend with better quiet,
> Better opinion, better confirmation,
> For all the soil of the achievement goes
> With me into the earth (4. 5. 130–131, 183–190).

Announcing the death of his father, Hal, the new King, draws attention to the affinities between father and son. After saying, 'My father is gone wild into his grave', he adds,

> For in his tomb lie my affections,
> And with his spirits sadly I survive,
> To mock the expectation of the world (5. 2. 123–126).

Consequently, the forces of disorder and anarchy must be put down, beginning with Falstaff, who represents Hal's (now Henry V) past. Indeed, the play is pervaded with the theme of mutability. Time is continually referred to. Hastings, the rebel based upon Lord Ralph Hastings (d. 1405), a minor nobleman from the north of Yorkshire, at the end of the first act aptly and prophetically observes, 'We are time's subjects, and time bids be gone' (1. 3. 110). Historically, following the Battle of Shrewsbury, the King controlled the country for at least a decade. In this play, he is depicted as old, sick and tired. His son Hal is increasingly aware that if he lingers in the bars too long, he will 'profane the precious time' (2. 4. 362). Falstaff, too, is no longer what he was. His entrance in the play in the second scene consists of him asking his page what the doctor has noted concerning the urine he sent him (1. 2. 1–2). To Doll Tearsheet he admits, 'I am old, I am old' (2. 4. 271). There is an elegiac autumnal quality to the play. The gullible, garrulous old, rural Gloucestershire Justice of the Peace Shallow, who knew Falstaff in his better days, observes 'Death, as the Psalmist saith, is certain to all, all shall die' (3. 2. 36–37). Images of disease, sickness, mortality, ageing reverberate throughout *Henry IV Part 2*.

Another element of the play, and one that is to dominate *Henry V* too, is the metaphor of the theatre, performance, play acting, revealed through rhetoric. The dividing lines between the actual and fantasy, the true and the untrue, are frequently blurred. *Henry IV Part 2* opens with the figure of 'Rumour [in a robe] painted full of tongues.' This is 'a personification possibly based on Virgil's "Fama", depicted as a female monster with many eyes, ears, and tongues who circulated both true and false accounts of events. See *Aeneid* 4. 179–190' (*Norton*: 1334, n. 1). Indeed, in the opening lines, Rumour admonishes the audience, 'Open your ears; for which of you will stop the | The vent of hearing when loud Rumour speaks?' Rumour points to deliberate deception clothed in misleading language, 'I speak of peace, while covert enmity | Under the smile of safety wounds the world' (Induction: 1–2, 9–10). In other words, language is full of ambiguity, as is human activity: what seems to be so is not.

Falstaff revels in double and treble meanings. For instance, in the second scene, Falstaff is angry at the rich merchant who will not give him satin without sufficient guarantees to ensure that he is paid back. Falstaff tells his page: 'Well, he may sleep in security, for he hath the horn of abundance, and the lightness of his wife shines through it; and yet cannot he see, though he have his own lanthorn to light him.' In this context, language certainly has multiple layers of meaning. 'Horn' could first be a reference to a commodity, a type of lantern sold by a merchant; secondly, it can refer to a cuckold, to the horns traditionally depicting a man whose wife has betrayed him; thirdly, it can refer to the merchant's own sleeping sexual organ. Similarly, 'lightness' (1. 2. 45–49) can imply his wife's promiscuity and/or her radiance. In this play, the language of the taverns is mostly physical and sexual, while the language of the King is elaborate and poetically inflated to contrast with the suggestive prose of the taverns.

Henry IV Part 2 concludes with a prose 'Epilogue' addressed to the audience. Whether deception is intended or not, contrary to the 'Epilogue's' claim – 'If you [the audience] be not too much cloy'd with the fat meat, our humble author will continue the story with Sir John in it' (26–28) – Falstaff is not present in *Henry V*. His death, however, is described in most moving prose by Mistress Quickly in Act 2, scene 3 of the play: she is 'sure, he's not in hell' (9 and see 10–26). The 'Epilogue' to *Henry IV Part 2* does admit however, that the historical 'Oldcastle' upon whom Falstaff is based 'died [a] martyr, and this is not the man', that is, not Falstaff (32).

Henry V

Henry V is the final play of Shakespeare's Second Tetralogy, or the *Richard II, Henry IV Parts 1 and 2* and *Henry V* cycle of plays, the First Tetralogy being his initial four plays based upon English history: the three *Henry VI* dramas and *Richard III*. First printed in the 1600 Quarto that claims to have been 'sundry times played by the Right honourable the Lord Chamberlaine his seruants', the 1623 folio edition of the play is more than double that of the Quarto one with 3,381 lines contrasted with 1,622 lines. The important chorus is omitted from the earlier Quarto version of the play, and some of the chorus's lines most probably refer specifically to contemporary events such as 'the General' Essex's return in disgrace on 28 September 1599 from a failed Irish campaign (5. 0. 30–5).

Indeed, the very presence of the Chorus in what appears to be suppressed passages at the time of the early performances indicate one of the central concerns and metaphors of the play, that of the theatre. The play is replete with theatrical language, from its very first word 'O' indicating the symmetry of the theatre in which it was being performed ('O' can also refer to the creative womb), to the Chorus's last speech in which the Chorus refers to 'In little room confining mighty men'. His final line, the final line of the play, is an appeal to the theatrical and reading audience: 'In your fair minds let this acceptance take' (5. 0. 3, 14). In the third line of the play, the Chorus specifically refers to 'A kingdom for a stage, princes to act.' He asks the audience and the reader

Can this cockpit hold
The vasty fields of France? Or may we cram

Within this wooden O [the theatre or creative womb/
    imagination] the very casques [helmets]
That did affright the air at Agincourt ? (1. 0. 11–14).

The Agincourt allusion is to a specific historical event. Its source is
Holinshed and Henry VIII's historian Edward Halle (*c.*1498–1547),
for whom he wrote *The Union of the Two Noble and Illustrious Families of Lancaster and York* (1548). In this work, Halle praises the
Tudors and exposes the dangers of civil war and the consequences of
regicide and the fear of divine retribution. With the anonymous
drama *The Famous Victories of Henry V* (1598), these sources dwelt
upon the significance of Henry's Agincourt victory in 1415, on his
personal bravery seemingly against overwhelming French odds. These
aspects are represented in *Henry V* by his rallying rhetorical forensic
speech before Agincourt to his soldiers with its appeal to bravery,
unity and historical memory (4. 3. 18–67). All this bravery and
nationalism is undercut at the end of the play when the Chorus refers
to Henry's successor, his infant son, Henry VI's advisors, 'Whose
state so many had the managing, | That they lost France, and made
his England bleed' (5. 0. 11–12).

Young Henry is noted as having 'sweet and honeyed sentences'
(1. 1. 50). In Act 2, Scene 2, he rhetorically entraps the traitors
Scrope (*c.*1376–1415), Cambridge (d. 1415) and Grey (d. 1415).
They advise Henry not to display mercy towards a common drunk.
Henry shows mercy, but not to the three traitors. Before the siege
of Harfleur, another actual siege that took place (1415), Henry's
linguistic games are significant. At the gates of the town, he delivers
to its leading citizens an outline of the terrors awaiting its inhabitants
if their governor does not surrender the city. He refers to 'her ashes'
and 'The gates of mercy shall be all shut up,' to rape and murder 'The
blind and bloody soldier with foul hand' that will '[Defile] the locks
of your shrill-shrieking daughters', to 'Your naked infants spitted
upon pikes' (3. 3. 9–10, 34–35, 38). Such language has its desired
effect. The city surrenders without bloodshed.

Language is not to be trusted in this play. In its opening scenes,
Henry's Archbishops pursue specious arguments and self-interest
in order to persuade Henry to invade France. Pistol pretends to
be brave. He describes Bardolph as 'a soldier firm and sound of

heart, | Of buxom valor' (3. 6. 26–27). Both are shown to be thieves and cowards. There, too, is tremendous dialect variation in the play: English, Irish, Scottish and Welsh. Nim indulges in constant repetition; Mistress Quickly revels in malapropisms. A whole scene (3. 4) is in French, and most of another, an important courtship scene in which Henry speaks English and Katherine speaks French and partial English, is in both languages or in attempts at both languages (5. 2), with the outcome a foregone conclusion.

The emphasis upon the theatrical, the mistrust of language, the pointlessness of Henry's invasion, serve to reinforce the sense of illusion underlying the play. Of course, it conforms to the pattern of the other historical plays. *Henry V* is as concerned as the others with recent English history; it is based on the Chronicle plays, contains spectacle, pageantry, and battles, assumes that Kings can do what they like, and that they have a Divine Right to execute and to invade. The play is concerned with order, with a fear of chaos, with the dangers of a power vacuum. In this way, it reflects the uncertain period in which it was written, the last years of Queen Elizabeth's reign. Some of its major themes are order and disorder, the threat to those in power, war and its consequences, the testing of a monarch – what makes a King – the business of honour and what it constitutes, illusion and reality represented for instance by the metaphor of the theatre, mutability (time past, present and future), how history is perceived and the fundamental issue of personal survival and male bonding. In this way, *Henry V* contains much that is present also in Shakespeare's tragedies.

Chapter Six
The Tragedies

Shakespeare's tragedies are an essential part of his great creative period. There are eleven plays in the *First Folio* categorized as 'Tragedies'. The final one, *Cymbeline*, is today regarded as a 'romance'. Unlike the other ten plays, it ends happily. The ten tragedies extend from Shakespeare's earliest creative period to his mature and greatest dramas.

Titus Andronicus

The first, the gruesome *Titus Andronicus* is found in a Quarto form in 1594. Henslowe's diary records that a drama named 'titus & ondrinicus' was performed at the Rose Theatre on 24 January 1594. The theatre was subsequently closed owing to the plague. Shortly following its closure, the play was entered in the Stationers' Register on 6 February 1594. There is a scholarly consensus that Shakespeare wrote it in collaboration. The play is noteworthy for its depiction of rape and various acts of horrific violence. Its focus upon elements of gender, race and sexuality resulted in a revival of interest in the play in the late twentieth and early twenty-first century.

Romeo and Juliet

With its depiction of young love, family and generational conflict, *Romeo and Juliet* is one of Shakespeare's most well-known tragedies and is often a person's first encounter with a Shakespeare play. *Romeo and Juliet* initially appeared in the Quarto edition in 1597. According to its title page, the tragedy has 'been often (with great applause) played publicly, by the right Honourable Lord Hunsdon his servants'. On 17 March 1597, Shakespeare's company became the Lord Chamberlain's Men, so the Quarto appeared earlier than that date. However, between 9 February and 2 March 1597, the printer's presses were seized. In the opening act of the play, there is probably a contemporary allusion that assists in dating the drama. The Nurse observes, "'Tis since the earthquake now eleven years' (1. 3. 23). This has been taken to allude to an earthquake that occurred in England in 1584. A second Quarto edition of 'The Most Excellent and Lamentable Tragedy of Romeo and Juliet' was published in 1599, 'newly corrected, augmented and amended', testifying to the contemporary popularity of this play which has rarely been out of the repertory.

Julius Caesar

The third tragedy focusing on the themes of honour, politics and the killing of a ruler, set in classical Rome, 'The Tragedy of Julius Caesar' only appears in printed form in the 1623 *First Folio*. Thomas Platter (1574–1628), a Swiss physician, visited England from 18 September to 20 October 1599. On 21 September, he records that he saw *Julius Caesar* played 'with approximately fifteen characters [in] the straw-thatched house' (Chambers: I: 397, II: 322), probably the Globe. Consequently, it probably was one of the earliest of Shakespeare's plays to be performed at the new theatre following the 1599 transfer of the company to their new venue.

Hamlet

Then follows the great sequence of Shakespeare's mature tragedies. A date is extremely difficult to assign to 'The Tragedy of Hamlet, Prince of Denmark'. A play entitled *The Revenge of Hamlet Prince [of] Denmark* 'lately acted by the Lord Chamberlain his servants' appears in the July 1602 Stationers' Register. '*The Tragical Historie of Hamlet,*

Prince of Denmarke by William Shake-speare. As it hath beene diuerse times acted by his Highnesse seruants in the City of London: as also in the two Vuniuersities of Cambridge and Oxford, and elsewhere.' It was published as a Quarto in 1603 and printed in London, probably by Valentine Simmes (active 1576–1622), printer of early editions of Shakespeare's plays, in fact nine in seven years. The reference to 'his Highnesse seruants' points to a post-19 May 1603 publication, the date on which the Lord Chamberlain's Company came under the patronage of the new monarch, James I.

Francis Meres in 1598 does not list *Hamlet*, although the poet, pamphleteer and annotator Gabriel Harvey (*c.*1550–1631) mentions having seen what must have been a very early performance of the play. In an undated passage, he comments, 'The younger sort takes much delight in Shakespeares Venus, & Adonis: but his Lucrece, & his tragedie of Hamlet, Prince of Denmarke, haue it in them, to please the wiser sort.' This observation must have been written following his acquisition of a copy of Thomas Speght's (d. 1621),1598 edition of Chaucer's *Works* in which it is found (cited *Riverside*: 1965).

At any rate, probably late in 1604, a second Quarto printed by the London printer James Roberts (fl. 1564–1608) appeared. The title page claims that it is 'Newly imprinted and enlarged to almost as much againe as it was, according to the true and perfect Coppie'. This implies defects, errors in the first Quarto and the second Quarto is different and almost twice as long as the first. In the earlier Quarto, there are even different character names, for example, Polonius is Corambis and Reynaldo is Montano. The famous 'To be or not to be' soliloquy found in the *First Folio* of 1623, and in almost the same version in the second Quarto, is radically different in the first Quarto. The opening lines reading, 'To be, or not to be, I there's the point, | To Die, to sleepe, is that all? I all' becomes for 'To be, or not to be, that is the question: | Whether 'tis nobler in the mind to suffer . . .' (3. 1. 56–57). In short, the first Quarto presents many problems and only two copies are known to have survived. One lacking the final leaf is today in the Huntington Library, San Marino, Southern California. The other, lacking its title page, is in the British Library in London. Seven copies of the 1604 second Quarto survive. Three dated 1604 are today in the United States: the Folger Library,

Washington, DC; the Huntington, and the Elizabethan Club Collection at the Beinecke Library at Yale University. Four, dated 1604, are today at the British Library, Trinity College at Cambridge, the Bodleian Library at Oxford, and at the University of Wroclaw in Poland.

Modern editions of *Hamlet* are based upon the second Quarto and the 1623 Folio printing. Ann Thompson and Neil Taylor in their 2006 Arden edition publish 'fully modernized and edited versions of all three texts'. In their 'Introduction', they write, 'The only features that these three *Hamlets* have in common are the name and designation of the chief character, and the fact that they are plays. But each is connected with one of the other two, whether through its printer, its publisher, its author or its acting company.' They add, 'The textual history of *Hamlet* is full of questions and largely empty of clear answers' (xvii, 76). In this way, it is akin to Shakespeare's own biography.

In addition to Harvey's undated reference to the play, there are internal allusions that have attracted scholarly interest concerning the dating of *Hamlet*, and especially its affinities to *Julius Caesar*. The first scene of *Hamlet* refers to

In the most high and palmy state of Rome,
A little ere the mightiest Julius fell,
The graves stood tenantless, and the sheeted dead
Did squeak and gibber in the Roman streets. (113–116)

Polonius in the second scene of the third act replies to Hamlet's 'What did you enact?' ironically, in view of his own stabbing by Hamlet: 'I did enact Julius Caesar. I was kill'd in' th' Capitol; Brutus kill'd me' (102–104). *Julius Caesar* was probably performed at the Globe on 21 September 1599, if the contemporary eyewitness Thomas Platter is to be believed, so *Hamlet* probably belongs to a subsequent date and there is speculation 'that the roles of Caesar and Brutus in' *Julius Caesar* first performed in 1599 'were taken by the same actors as now played Polonius and Hamlet' (Jenkins, ed., *Hamlet*: 294 n 103).

In addition to the close relationship between the two plays, there are also parallels between *Hamlet* and John Marston's (?1575–1634) *Antonio's Revenge*. This play is found entered in the Stationers' Register on 24 October 1601. Both thematically are preoccupied with revenge and its consequences; there are also verbal echoes between them. Scholars including E. K. Chambers (1866–1954) and Harold Jenkins (1909–2000), have also drawn attention to the boy actors performing at the Black Friars from Michaelmas (September–October) 1600. They performed in Ben Jonson's *Cynthia's Revels* before the end of 1600 and in the following year in his *Poetaster*. In both, there are taunts at the expense of older, professional performers which scholars have referred to as a 'so-called "war of the theatres"' (Thompson and Taylor, ed., *Hamlet*: 52–53).

In the second scene of Act 2 of *Hamlet*, there are references to 'little eyasas' [unfledged hawks] that are 'now the fashion' and 'berattle the common stages' and to the 'throwing about of brains' (339, 341–341, 358–359). Interestingly, such allusions to boy actors are absent from the second Quarto while they are present in the first Quarto and in the Folio. Absent in the first Quarto but present in the second Quarto and in the Folio is a reference in the second scene of the second act to 'the late innovation' (2. 2. 296 in Quarto 2). Both Harold Jenkins in his Arden edition and John Dover Wilson, the earlier twentieth-century Shakespearean scholar-critic and author of *The Manuscript of Shakespeare's Hamlet* (1934) and *What Happens in Hamlet* (1935), argue that these words are an allusion to the abortive Essex rebellion against Queen Elizabeth of 8 February 1601.

It is far too easy to be sidetracked in discussion of *Hamlet*, a play that has generated far more written reactions in diverse languages and cultures than any other Shakespearean text. Before turning to a brief account of the dates of the other tragedies, one further fact should be noted. The first actual record that has survived of a specific performance indicates it took place not in London or even on land, but on board a ship anchored off the African coast on 5 September 1607 on the appropriately named *Red Dragon*. Its captain, William Keeling, took refuge in a storm off what is today known as the coast of Sierra Leone. His journal records for that day: 'We gave the tragedie of Hamlet.' Again, on 31 September, he invited a fellow captain 'to a fish dinner and had Hamlet acted abord . . . w[hi]ch I p[er]mit to keepe my people from idelness and unlawful games or sleep' (cited Thompson and Taylor, ed., *Hamlet*: 54). Even for those at sea, *Hamlet* has its universal appeal with its great poetry focused upon, to mention just a few of its preoccupations: revenge, indecision, mother and son relationships, insanity, the rational and irrational, suspicion, treachery and deceit.

Othello

According to the accounts of the Office of the Revels, *The Tragedy of Othello the Moore of Venice* was performed at James I's court on 1 November 1604 at the Banqueting House at Whitehall. The Office of the Revels was created to arrange Christmas and Easter court entertainments. Its role after the 1580s increasingly became one of licensing and censorship, as the players began to control their own productions. Echoes of the play may be found in a 1604 drama by Thomas Dekker and Thomas Middleton (1580–1627), *The Honest Whore*. The information on the Turkish invasion of Cyprus and the Turkish navy found in *Othello* most probably originates in Richard Knolles' (*c.*1545–1610) *The General History of the Turks*, published at its very earliest by 30 September 1603. This work is regarded as the earliest major account of the Ottoman Empire and its navy. It was dedicated to James I and VI of Scotland. So, Shakespeare most probably wrote the tragedy between October 1603 and the autumn of 1604. A Quarto version did not appear until 1622. The subsequent 1623 Folio version is approximately 160 lines longer and there over 1,000 wording variants between the two. The 1623 Folio includes Desdemona's willow song (4. 3) and additional lines for Emilia in the closing parts. The 1622 Quarto version has fuller stage directions and over fifty oaths. These may well have been cut out of the 1623 Folio as a reaction to the 1606 Profanity Act or Act to Restrain Abuse of Players. This levied a fine of 10 pounds on an actor uttering the name of God or Jesus Christ in vain.

Othello was performed frequently at court and at different theatres until they were closed at the outbreak of the Civil War in 1642. During Shakespeare's own lifetime, the play seems to have been among the most performed of his dramas and subsequently has retained its popularity. Eleven films have been made of it, and it has been the inspiration for various operas, including Gioachimo Rossini's (1792–1868) 1816 version and Verdi's *Otello* of 1887, with libretto by Arrigo Boito (1842–1918).

Timon of Athens

Karl Marx (1818–1883) regarded the money and value-obsessed, bitter, misanthropic tragedy of *Timon of Athens* as the most interesting among Shakespeare's works. He was particularly attracted to 'Timon's apostrophe to gold' in the third scene of the fourth act (lines 381–392), 'which stresses gold's power to invert values' (Dawson and Minton, eds, Arden ed., *Timon of Athens*: 71) and to 'sold'rest close close impossibilities' (l. 387). There are two key aspects of money that Marx '"sees unveiled in the passage." These are, first, the "visible divinity of money,"' its ability to transform 'all human and natural properties into their contraries' (Marx cited in Arden ed., 71). Secondly, its function as the 'common whore of mankind' (l. 43) of 'the world in empire' (l. 392). Indeed, 'the word "gold" is almost twice as common in *Timon* as in any other Shakespeare play, appearing 36 times' (Dawson and Minton, Arden ed.: 92 n 1).

Although the idea has been around since the 1830s, since the work of MacDonald P. Jackson (b. 1938) and others in the 1970s there has been general acceptance in the scholarly community today that the play is a collaborative one, with Thomas Middleton writing approximately one-third of it. The text is included in Gary Taylor and John Lavagnino's *Thomas Middleton: The Collected Works* (2007) under the title 'The Life of Timon of Athens' (467–508). Its first publication occurs in the 1623 *First Folio*, probably in the pages that were intended for *Troilus and Cressida*. The text is replete with plot loose ends and inconsistencies, especially in its pronoun usage. Its vocabulary has much in common with *King Lear* and might have been influenced by an anonymous drama *Timon*, performed at an Inn of Court around 1602–1603.

Timon of Athens doesn't seem to have been performed before the poet and dramatist Thomas Shadwell's (?1642–1692) adaptation, *The History of Timon of Athens, the Man-Hater* in 1678. The first sentence of Shadwell's 'Prefatory' observation that 'It has the inimitable hand of Shakespear in it, which never made more masterly strokes than this. Yet I can truly say, I have made it into a play', seems to represent a general consensus. Shadwell's addition of a love plot 'extending the play's opposition between loyal servants and false friends by supplying Timon with a loyal mistress . . . and an affected mercenary fiancée Melissa' (Dobson and Wells: 476–477), has not found such uniformity of opinion.

Macbeth

The Scottish tragedy, on the other hand, is among its author's greatest works and easier to assign a probable date to. Modern textual scholarship detects the hands of Thomas Middleton in, for instance, the two songs with the opening phrases 'Come away, come away, etc' and 'Black Spirits, etc' (3. 5. and 4. 1. of the 1623 Folio: the one in which the text first appeared). Exactly the same words are found in Middleton's *The Witch* (*c*.1613).

The text of the *First Folio* is unsatisfactory. It is very short. In *Macbeth*, Hecat personally appears before the Witches in Act 3, Scene 5 and Act 4, Scene 1 without having a real plot consequence. There is also the famous drunken porter appearance immediately following murder and high tragedy. These occurrences suggest deliberate textual omission in order to protect the dramatic text from piracy. In other words, during a performance, a 'pirate' from a rival theatrical company was spotted in the house transcribing the text and the performance details. These were immediately altered in order to thwart the pirate and the rival company. In spite of these textual problems, an astute critic such as A. C. Bradley (1851–1935), in his influential *Shakespearean Tragedy* (1904), includes the play, along with *Hamlet*, *Othello* and *King Lear*, as one of the 'great tragedies' and observes that 'almost all the scenes which at once recur to the memory take place either at night or in some dark spot' (cited *Riverside*: 1355).

The play's concern with its Scottish setting and history, witches, spirits and witchcraft, a subject on which the new monarch considered himself an authority – he wrote a work on the subject called *Daemonologie,* published in 1599 – and the appearance of Banquo, the King's ancestor, strongly suggests that *Macbeth* was written with King James, the patron of the King's (formerly Lord Chamberlain's) Men, in mind. In the sources, Banquo is an accomplice in Duncan's murder. In Shakespeare's play, he is not. This is probably a ploy by the dramatist to please the new monarch. Indeed, the dramatic witches conjure up for Macbeth an apparition extending for eight generations of subsequent Scottish monarchs. All are Banquo's descendants and consequently bring the drama to the present, as James's mother Mary Stuart is the eighth generation and King James is the eighth monarch in lineage succeeding to the throne. For many commentators, the witches' words at the conclusion of their ceremonies to 'show the best of our delights . . . | That this great king may kindly say | Our duties did his welcome pay' indicate that the play was performed before 'this great king' (4. 1. 127–132), James I.

There also is a consensus for a 1606 dating for its first performances, with a probable date of composition between 1603, the year of James's accession to the throne following the death of Elizabeth on 24 March 1603, and 1606. In 1607, *The Puritan* was published. Probably by Middleton, it alludes to *Macbeth* and to Banquo's ghost. In Act, I, Scene III of Shakespeare's play there is an allusion to 'the Tiger' and to eighty-one weeks of storms (7, 25). An actual ship of that name arrived at Milford Haven in June 1606, following a tempestuous voyage of exactly the same duration. Further, the porter in scene three of the second act refers to 'here's an equivocator, that could swear in both the scales against either scale, who committed treason enough for God's sake, yet could not equivocate to heaven. O, come in, equivocator' (2. 3. 8–10). The context is the murder of King Duncan: 'Most sacrilegious murther' (67). The threefold play on 'equivocator' (8–10) probably refers to the events of November 1605, when a group of Catholic conspirators led by Robert Catesby (1573–1605) and Guy Fawkes (1570–1606), a mining expert, attempted unsuccessfully to blow up the Houses of Parliament – celebrated to this day as Guy Fawkes or Bonfire Night – on 5 November 1605. In 1606, the Jesuit Henry Garnet (1555–1606), the author of a defense of equivocation for persecuted Catholics, was tried for involvement in the plot.

The earliest known record of performance of the play to have survived is by Simon Forman who describes a Globe performance of Saturday 20 April 1611. His account is curious as it contains errors. For instance, there is no cauldron scene and Macbeth doesn't become the Prince of Northumberland. Forman describes Macbeth and Banquo as 'riding through a wood' although, in spite of the relative sophistication of the Globe theatrical devices, it is unlikely, although not improbable, that the Globe actors would have been riding horses.

Forman recalls, 'The ghoste of Banco came and sate down in his cheier behind [Macbeth]. And he turninge About to sit down Again sawe the goste of Banco, which fronted him so, that he fell into a great passion of fear and fury' (cited *Norton*: 3309).

Forman's eyewitness account almost conjures up the great poetic characteristics of this play and of Shakespeare's great tragedies. An astute twentieth-century commentator Frank Kermode (1919–), in his *Shakespeare's Language* (2000), observes that, 'It is surely impossible to deny that certain words – "time," "man," "done" – and certain themes – "blood," "darkness" – are the matrices of the language of the play'. Kermode adds, 'In the period of the great tragedies these matrices appear to have been fundamental to Shakespeare's procedures.'

King Lear

Kermode's 'matrices' (215) are certainly present in the tragedy which the great Shakespearean critic Dr Johnson 'could hardly bear to read to its conclusion' (Kermode: 197). According to the Stationers' Register of 26 November 1607, *King Lear* was performed at court on 26 December 1606. The poetic funeral elegy from 1619 for the renowned tragic actor Richard Burbage speaks of his 'Kind Leer' (Dobson and Wells: 58). The drama probably was written between the spring of 1603 and the autumn of 1606. One of its chief sources, Samuel Harsnett's (1561–1631) exposure of exorcist practices called *A Declaration of Egregious Popish Impostures*, has extensive structural as well as symbolic resemblances with *King Lear*. Harsnett's work appeared in 1603 and contains the names of the 'foul fiends' appearing in *King Lear*. Edgar dressed as the mad beggar, 'Poor Tom', claims to be possessed by them in Act 3, Scene 4 (129–140). A play influenced by Shakespeare's tragedy by Edward Sharpham (1576–1608), the *Fleir,* appears in the Stationers' Register for 13 May1606. It includes a scene very similar to that in which Lear allows a disguised Kent back into his service (1. 4).

Other contemporary allusions serve to limit the play to the 1603–1606 period. In the second scene of the first act, Gloucester tells Edmund, 'These late eclipses in the sun and moon pretend no good to us' (103–104). Scholars such as G. B. Harrison (1894–1991) argue that this is a reference to the eclipses of 7 September and 2 October 1605 (*Riverside*: 1298). 'Lunar and solar eclipses' witnessed 'in London about a year' prior to 'the play's first recorded perform-ance' on 26 December 1606 'would have added spice to [the] superstitious belief in the role of heavenly bodies as augers of misfor-tune'. Also, a lawsuit of late 1603 has close parallels to a central strand of the plot of *King Lear*. In this case, the two older daughters of an aging 'Sir Brian Annesley attempted to get their father legally certified as insane, thereby enabling themselves to take over his estate.' In the meantime, the younger daughter named Cordell (rather than Cordelia) strongly defended her father (*Norton*: 2502 n 4; 2326).

The textual history of the play is very complex and controversial. It was first published in a Quarto edition (Q1) during December 1607 and January 1608 at the shop of a London printer, Nicholas Okes (d. 1645) for the publisher Nathaniel Butter (d. 1664). Twelve copies of this Quarto are extant, but contain ten differing texts. Butter's shop was 'at the signe of the Pide Bull' and this Quarto is known as the 'Pied Bull Quarto'. The most informative title page reads:

> M William Shak-speare. His True Chronicle Historie of the life and death of King Lear and his three Daughters. With the vnfortunate life of Edgar, sonne and heire to the Earle of Gloster, and his sullen and assumed humor of Tom of Bedlam: As it was played before the Kings Maiestie at Whitehall vpon S. Stephans night in Christmas Hollidayes. By his Majesties seruants played vsually at the Gloabe on the Bancke-side. London, Printed for Nathaniel Butter, and are to be sold at his shop in Pauls Church-yard at the signe of the Pide Bull neere St. Austins Gate. 1608.

A subsequent Quarto (Q2) appeared dated apparently in 1608 and was attributed to Butter. Actually it belongs to the year 1619 and only slightly corrects some of the spelling, punctuation, words and phrases of Q1. An almost totally different version is found in the 1623 *First Folio*. There are many corrections, with expanded stage directions, over 300 lines of extra dialogue and roughly a hundred lines not in Q1. For instance, in the Q1, a line in the opening scene, 'Here's France and Burgundy, my noble lord,' is assigned to Gloucester (188). In the Folio, it becomes Cordelia's (*Norton*: 185). More importantly, lines such as Lear's last lines, 'Do you see this? Look on her. Look, her lips. | Look there, look there,' are found only in the Folio version (311–312). The convention at the beginning of the twenty-first century is to publish separately the texts, alongside one another, or the Q text under its original title as 'The History of King Lear' with its twenty four scenes and the F text as the 'Tragedy of King Lear' with its five acts and three scenes. The Norton edition, for example, 'presents Q1 and F on facing pages so that readers can compare them easily.' It also offers 'a conflated version . . . so that readers can encounter the tragedy in the form that it assumed in most editions from the eighteenth century until very recently' (2333).

Antony and Cleopatra

Shakespeare returns to ancient and to non-British history for *Antony and Cleopatra*, to the Roman Empire and its territories. The play was entered in the Stationers' Register for 20 May 1608, although it seems not to have been published until the *First Folio* of 1623. Except for the first scene of the opening act, neither act nor scene divisions are indicated in the *First Folio*. Modern texts tend to follow the act and scene divisions drawn up by Nicholas Rowe (1674–1718) in his six-volume edition of Shakespeare published in 1709. Curiously, no stage performance is recorded prior to 1759, when David Garrick (1717–1779) and Edward Capell (1731–1781) prepared a heavily revised version. John Dryden's (1631–1700) post-Restoration adaptation, with its wonderful title *All for Love; or, The World Well Lost* (1678), serves to highlight just how magnificent Shakespeare's poetry is compared with that of his imitators.

Shakespeare's use of one of his major sources of the play, Sir Thomas North's (1535–?1603) translation of Plutarch's *Lives of the Noble Greeks and Romans* (1579, second edition 1595), is displayed at its finest in, for instance, Shakespeare's transfiguration of North's prose description of Cleopatra's barge:

the poop whereof was of gold, the sails of purple, and the oars of silver which kept stroke in rowing after the sound of music of flutes, hautboys, cithens, viols . . . And now for the person of herself, she was laid under a pavilion of cloth of gold of tissue, apparelled and attired like the goddess Venus commonly drawn in picture; and hard by her, on either hand of her, pretty fair boys apparelled as painters do set forth god Cupid, with little fans on their hands. (cited *Riverside*: 1391)

Enobarbus, in the second scene of the second act, relates

> The barge she sat in, like a burnish'd throne,
> Burnt on the water. The poop was beaten gold,
> Purple the sails, and so perfumed that
> The winds were love-sick with them; the oars were silver,
> Which to the tune of flutes kept stroke, and made
> The water which they beat to follow faster,
> As amorous of their strokes. For her own person,
> It beggar'd all description: she did lie
> In her pavilion-cloth of gold, of tissue-
> O'er-picturing that Venus where we see
> The fancy outwork nature. On each side her
> Stood pretty dimpled boys, like smiling Cupids,
> With divers-color'd fans, whose wind did seem
> To [glow] the delicate cheeks which they did cool,
> And what they undid did (191–204).

The great twentieth-century literary critic F. R. Leavis (1895–1978), in his comparative analysis of Shakespeare's *Antony and Cleopatra* and Dryden's version, regards the latter's art as that of the 'stated' and Shakespeare's as 'presented or enacted'. Dryden's description is given to Antony: 'She came from Egypt. | Her Gally down the Silver Cydons row'd, | The Tackling Silk, her Streamers wav'd with Gold' and so on. For Leavis, 'Dryden's version offers in itself little lodgment for detailed commentary, and must service mainly as a foil to the Shakespearean passage' (Leavis: 160–161).

Certainly, neither North nor Dryden can compete with Shakespeare's wonderful use of cumulative, resonating assonance and alliteration in Enobarbus's description of Cleopatra's sensual progress down the Nile. Even Hollywood or scenic pictorial depictions cannot conjure up the imaginative sensuality of movement conveyed by Shakespeare at his greatest. Late twentieth-century and early twenty first-century students of Shakespeare's style detect in *Antony and Cleopatra* 'a major stylistic departure from its immediate predecessors' such as *Macbeth* and *King Lear* (Dobson and Wells: 15). *Antony and Cleopatra* is 'The work that appears to have liberated Shakespeare's imagination and moved him beyond the professional impasse that seems to be implicit in *King Lear* or *Timon*' (McDonald, *Shakespeare Later Style*: 106). For Adelman, the play has 'interpretive openness . . . expansive playfulness . . . imaginative abundance' (191–192).

In his *Shakespeare's Language*, Kermode, too, indicates its thematic, structural and 'striking' rhetorical difference from the other tragedies (217–218). Thematically, it focuses upon world history rather than the provincial or Roman history. The drama is a continual reminder of the transformation brought about by Octavius's victory at Actium where Antony loses 'half the bulk o' th' world' (3. 11. 64). The play hovers around reverberations of the word 'become' which, with its derivatives, occurs 'seventeen times . . . as against three times in *Lear*, six times in *Macbeth*, four times in *Timon*, nine in *Coriolanus*' and once only in the form of 'became' in *Hamlet* (Kermode: 218). It exhibits Shakespeare's later style in for instance its 'rapid switch from the seasonal imagery to that of the dolphin leaping out of the sea again' seen in Cleopatra's revelation of her dream of the emperor to Dolabella (5. 2. 81–92). This style is characterized not by a 'laborious working out of the figures, instead a sort of impatience at the unexplored resources of language' (Kermode: 229) including the revelling in the sheer sensuous qualities of language.

Such perceptions of the play representing a change in Shakespeare's style constitute a critical consensus but are speculative. *Antony and Cleopatra* is one of its author's lengthiest plays, with more than 3,000 lines and a high quality of very short scenes with the action moving rapidly over the Mediterranean world. Its impact appears to have been instant. Samuel Daniels' revision of his *Cleopatra* (1594) was published in 1607 and contains echoes of the language of Shakespeare's tragedy. Similarly, Barnabe Barnes's (1571–1609) *The Devil's Charter*, performed by the King's Men in February 1607, echoes Shakespeare. In Barnes's play, 'Alexander Borgia uses asps, which he calls "Cleopatraes birds," to poison two boys' (Chambers: I: 478).

Coriolanus

Set at another period of Roman history and also, like *Antony and Cleopatra,* based on Plutarch's *Lives* in Thomas North's translation, *The Tragedy of Coriolanus* seems to lack the same qualitative status as Shakespeare's other great tragedies. It is regarded as the most political of its author's plays and the last of the tragedies. First published in the *First Folio* of 1623, it contains detailed stage directions (see for example 1. 1 and 5. 2. 183), different speech headings such as 'Cor.', 'Corio' and 'Coriol', and inconsistent spellings such as 'Sc' for 'S' in the name of one of the Roman tribunes, 'Sicinius'. There are other irregularities, too, leading to the speculation that the Folio text 'probably derives either from a prompt book transcribed from foul papers, or from a transcript of such a prompt book.' Foul papers refer to the presumed rough drafts made by the dramatist prior to rehearsal. The prompt book was the officially approved text in which 'the book-keeper would have actors' parts copied', some stage directions and so on (Dobson and Wells: 90, 151, 347).

In the text, musical stage directions refer to cornets and the Folio text is divided into acts. These suggest that *Coriolanus* may well have been written or performed for the indoors Blackfriars Theatre run by the King's Men syndicate that included Shakespeare from August 1608, although an outbreak of the plague suspended use of the theatre until late in 1609. After this, the King's Men utilized the open-air Globe during the summer months and the indoor theatre in the winter. The year 1605 points to the earliest date it could have been composed. The opening scene utilizes William Camden's (1551–1623) *Remains of a Greater Work Concerning Britain,* published in 1605. Here, Shakespeare would have found Menenius' fable of the belly (1. 1. 97). This fable is referred to in works by a dramatist associated with the King's Men, Shakespeare's company. It is found in, for instance, Robert Armin's drama, *The Italian Tailor and His Boy,* recorded in the Stationers' Register for February 1609. Another verbal echo is found in Ben Jonson's *Epicoene, or The Silent Women,* which was initially performed in 1609. In the play, the line 'You have lurch'd your friends of the better halfe of the garland' (5. 4. 227) echoes Cominius' tribute to Coriolanus: 'He lurched all swords of the garland' (2. 2. 101: cf. Chambers: I: 479).

If 1605 to 1609 seem to be terminal dates for the play's composition, there are in it allusions to English events that took place between 1607 and 1608, including a personal event of great importance to Shakespeare. His mother, Mary, was buried on 9 September 1608. It is speculation to suppose that the play's emphasis upon the role of the shrewd but ferocious Volumnia, the mother of Coriolanus, was influenced by personal matters affecting the playwright. But Shakespeare gives her a greater role than the character has in Shakespeare's main source for the play Thomas North's translation of Plutarch's 'Life of Caius Martius Coriolanus' in his *Lives of the Noble Greeks and Romans*.

In the opening scene of the play, the line 'the coal of fire upon the ice' (173), probably refers to the fact that for the first time for many years – in fact, since 1564–1565 – the River Thames froze over. On 8 January 1608, 'pans of coals' (Chambers: I: 479) burnt on it. The winter of 1607–1608 was especially harsh. Also in 1608 and 1609, there was a corn shortage, referred to in the opening scene of the play in the First citizen's reference to the ruling class: 'They ne'er car'd for us yet. Suffer us to famish, and their store-houses cramm'd with grain' (79–81). Indeed, the depiction in the play of the hostile relations between the plebeians and their aristocratic rulers may well reflect problems resulting from the 1607 rioting on the part of the agrarian poor in the midlands. These riots were the consequence of serious food shortages. Another contemporary allusion may well be found in Coriolanus's depiction of treachery in the opening scene of the third act: 'he'll turn your current in a ditch, | And make your channel his? If he have power' (96–97). This may well allude to Hugh Middleton's (*c.*1556–1631) highly publicized entrepreneurial efforts to carry water to the city of London by a new artificial river or canal completed early in 1609.

No evidence of a production of the play before the Restoration seems to have survived, apart from the allusions to the play in the dramas of Armin and Jonson. The first recorded production appears to be Nahum Tate's (1652–1715) adaptation performed in 1681. This, as its title suggests, *The Ingratitude of a Commonwealth*, places emphasis upon the theme of ingratitude on a political scale, which runs through Shakespeare's play. Tate's version is especially tragic and bloody. Coriolanus dies on stage as do his eventual murderer,

Aufidius, and Coriolanus's young son, Martius, and wife Virgilia. Volumnia, meanwhile, loses her mind.

In the twentieth century, fascist regimes used the play for their own purposes. In 1934, French fascists supported a production at the *Comédie Française*, stressing its total attack on democratic views. Such a perception was not confined to the fascists. In 1935 at the height of Stalinist rule, a performance in Moscow interpreted Coriolanus as an aristocratic enemy of the people. The Nazis performed the play frequently as a paean to strong, autocratic, dictatorial leadership. They found support for their interpretation in Coriolanus's lines revealing his distaste for democracy: 'where gentry, title, wisdom, | Cannot conclude but by the yea and no | Of general ignorance–' the social consequences are 'unstable slightness' (3. 1. 144–146, 148).

The period 1605–1609 was a particularly turbulent one in English politics. A new monarch had ascended to the throne. The King and his son Charles seemed allied with ideas of Imperial Rome and the perception of its authoritarian, dictatorial forms of government where the ruler's power was subject to little restraint. On the other hand, an increasingly vocal, powerful element in parliament and elsewhere allied themselves with a vision of a Roman Republic where power was dispersed between the consuls, the senate and the tribunes rather than being concentrated in the hands of a single ruler, Caesar. Already, the seeds of the Civil War that would break out in the 1640s were emerging, politically, economically and on religious lines. Various voices wished to see power dispersed between the monarch, the House of Lords and the House of Commons.

Coriolanus, as in its different way *Julius Caesar*, deals with complex concerns. *Coriolanus* opens with the plebeians' rebellion over the lack of corn in Rome. Individually, the citizens are reasonable; collectively, they turn from one idol to another, at one time exulting Coriolanus and at another despising him. In his turn, Coriolanus is exploited and manipulated by the tribunes. As inflation rises, as it did in the first decade of the seventeenth century, so does the political temperature and political manipulation. The Senate chooses Coriolanus to be the supreme ruler, the Consul, but the citizens refuse him the position. The Romans are unable to accept Coriolanus's pride (as many were unable to accept Julius Caesar's pride), his defiance and his contempt for them. Egged on by his mother, Volumnia, his patriotism proves to be his downfall. He is killed by his friend turned enemy, Aufidius, who says, 'our virtues | Lie in th' interpretation of the time,' that is, in the way we react to and exploit the events of the current moment. Further, 'One fire drives out one fire; one nail one nail; | Rights by rights fouler, strengths by strengths do fail' (4. 7. 49–50, 54–55).

Characteristics of the Tragedies

Coriolanus, with the obscene pun implicit in its title, is a play dealing in political paradoxes. It is Shakespeare's final tragedy and has much in common with Shakespeare's other tragedies. They all have certain common characteristics, having their origins in the ancient Greek tragedies by Aeschylus, Sophocles, Euripides and others and outlined in Aristotle's famous fourth century (BC) analysis in his *Poetics.* For Aristotle, tragedy consists of 'the imitation of an action that is serious and also, as having magnitude, complete in itself' expressed poetically and dramatically. It has 'incidents arousing pity and fear, wherewith to accomplish the catharsis of such emotions' (Abrams: 331). This idea of *catharsis,* purification or purgation is crucial. In other words, the tragic representation of suffering and death on the stage leaves the audience not ultimately depressed but relieved. Through experiencing the extreme plight of others, the audience finds relief: there but for the grace of God, go we. Not all accept such a view; indeed, the experience of the tragic can lead to identification with those suffering, or an attempt to prevent what is taking place. The great Dr. Samuel Johnson, for instance, approved Nahum Tate's changing of the ending of *King Lear* to a happy one in his 1681 adaptation *The History of King Lear.*

Essential to Shakespearean and Classical tragedy is the death of the leading central *protagonist* and protagonists. At the conclusion of *Hamlet,* for example, Horatio, Hamlet's close friend, the only one he is prepared to trust, is the only one around him to survive to tell his tale. Hamlet, in almost his final words, asks Horatio:

> If thou didst ever hold me in they heart,
> Absent thee from felicity awhile,

And in this harsh world draw they breath in pain
To tell my story (5. 2. 346–349).

Even in the harsh, bleak, cynical world of *Coriolanus,* there is a survivor remaining from the carnage to tell the story. In this instance, Aufidius, the erstwhile friend turned enemy, insists in the final words of the tragedy that Coriolanus be buried with full military honours: 'Yet he shall have a noble memory,' a 'noble' burial and memorial (5. 6. 154). In the final speech of *Hamlet*, the young Fortinbras, who has avenged his own father's death at the hands of Hamlet's father, also represents a new regime. He, too, insists that his enemy be buried with dignity: 'Let four captains | Bear Hamlet like a soldier to the stage . . . The soldiers' music and the rite of war | Speak loudly for him' (5. 2. 395–400).

Common to the tragedies is a *protagonist*, a chief character of high, noble birth who as a consequence of a series of actions undertaken by him/herself, results in a disastrous, catastrophic conclusion for others. Indeed, the essential difference between Shakespearean tragedy and his other work, such as the plays referred to in the *First Folio* as 'Comedies', is that the tragedies result in the death of the protagonist and those close to him/her. Central, too, is the idea of *hamartia* or error: a mistake of judgement or tragic flaw of the tragic hero or protagonist. Hamlet, for instance, delays too long: he is unable to make up his mind, to come to a decision. Julius Caesar ignores the warning signs; he has too much pride. Othello, in common with Coriolanus, is puffed with pride, and in the former's case, eaten up with jealousy and far too gullible. Macbeth listens to his wife too much and begins to enjoy killing; once he has murdered, he is unable to stop doing so. Lear, too, has too much pride and makes serious, tragic errors of judgement. He does not trust the one daughter who loves him, Cordelia, and irrationally, impulsively gives up his power too easily to those he mistakenly thinks he can trust.

Combined with *hamartia* is the classical idea of *hubris*. Shakespeare's tragic heroes possess in one form or another pride, an overweening self-confidence that leads them to disregard a divine warning or violate an important law. Hamlet, for instance, is warned by his father, in ghostly form, not to harm his mother. Macbeth does not pay close heed to the witches and too much attention to his wife's ambition and blood thirstiness. Timon of Athens is too misanthropic and he does not listen, although he recognizes the insight of Flavius, who remains loyal to him: 'I do proclaim | One honest man-mistake me not, but one; | No more, I pray-and he's a steward' (4. 3. 497–498). He cannot accept that there is more than a single honest person.

In addition to the classical, tragic formula of *catharsis*, the central protagonist who dies, *hamartia* and *hubris*, the tragedies have a tragic denouement. In tragedy, the denouement, or final unravelling, or unknotting, ends in catastrophe, in death. At the conclusion of *Hamlet*, for example, Hamlet dies; so do Claudius, Hamlet's mother, the Queen, and Laertes. The play ends in disaster, death for the protagonist, and a new regime takes over.

In addition to the classical models, Shakespearean tragedy and that of his contemporaries draws upon the work of Lucius Annaeus Seneca (*c*.4 BC–AD 65). The Roman dramatist and philosopher wrote at least nine tragedies. His style was highly influential in the England of the sixteenth century, especially his rhetoric, exemplified in individual utterances 'of a highly, wrought impassioned speech' (Dobson and Wells: 414).

Elements of the style are partially seen in the great *soliloquies* found in Shakespeare's tragedies but by no means confined to them. A character largely alone on stage, such as Hamlet, Lear, Othello or Macbeth, speaks his/her thoughts aloud to the unseen witnesses. Hamlet's 'To be or not to be' (3. 1. 55–89) soliloquy is the most famous example from many. Indeed, the soliloquies contain much of Shakespeare's finest poetry compressed into most magnificent lines of self expression and revelation. A character doesn't have to be alone: in some instances, an eavesdropper, of whom the speaker is unaware, overhears. An obvious example is the balcony scene in *Romeo and Juliet* when Romeo hears Juliet's speeches that are meant only for her. In another example, Hamlet sees Claudius praying and delivers his powerful soliloquy, 'Now might I do it pat, now a 'is a-praying' (3. 3. 73–96). This follows hard on the heels of Claudius's self revelation of guilt in his lengthy soliloquy, 'O my offence is rank! It smells to heaven' (3. 3. 36–72).[4]

Elizabethan dramatists such as Marlowe and Thomas Kyd revelled in Senecan scenes emphasizing incest, adultery, treachery, murder and above all, revenge, or the tragedy of blood. These dramas fully utilized murder, revenge, ghosts, physical mutilation, carnage and dead bodies littering the stage. There was a tremendous, an insatiable, Elizabethan appetite for violence, for the horrific. Thomas Kyd's *The Spanish Tragedy* (1586) for example, is a full-blown tragedy of blood with its full ingredients, including ghosts. It, too, begins with a ghost crying out for retribution. Hieronimo has lost his son, and, akin to Shakespeare's Hamlet, is extremely frustrated to the point of madness by his failure to obtain justice. His wife kills herself after, like Ophelia, she loses her reason. Heironimo, too, uses a play within a play to expose the guilt of the murderers. Subsequently, he bites out his own tongue and kills himself with a penknife. The demand for the gruesome did not stop with the death of Elizabeth. In fact, the Jacobeans perhaps revelled in the bloodthirsty and the gory even more, with their highly developed melodramas such as Thomas Middleton's *The Revenger's Tragedy* (1606). This revenge tragedy opens with Vindice the revenger holding a skull, vituperating the Duke and swearing revenge upon him and his family: 'Duke, royal lecher, go, grey-haired adultery | And thou his son, as impious steeped [evilly inclined] as he' (1. 1. 1–2: Middleton, *Collected Works*, 547).

Ghosts are not confined to *Hamlet* or the drama of Thomas Kyd. They reveal that the dramatist is drawing upon something that many members of the theatrical audience actually believed in. Even the hardened, sceptical experienced soldiers guarding the Danish kingdom at the start of *Hamlet* are disinclined to dismiss what they have actually seen appearing on the Elsinore ramparts and disappearing at dawn. The ghost of Hamlet's father appears and reappears at crucial times at the play. Even if some members of the audience are sceptical of a ghost's actual existence, the ghost represents deep inner recesses of the psyche or thought processes. Hamlet sees the ghost, but his mother Gertrude doesn't. On the battlements, the experienced, hardboiled soldiers physically witness the ghost who appears 'in the same figure like the King that's dead' and heralds 'some strange eruption to our state' (1. 1. 41, 69). The ghost acts as a prefiguring symbol of disruption: indeed, one of the key elements in the play is that 'Something is rotten in the state of Denmark' (1. 4. 89).

Hamlet and Shakespeare's other tragedies powerfully call into question the relationship between representation, theatrical stage appearance and reality. Hamlet struggles to verify the authenticity of the ghost through staging a play within a play and carefully observing the play's impact upon his uncle and mother. In doing so, he is drawing upon a religious and historical debate on ghosts with deep theological reverberations. To generalize, for most sixteenth-century Catholics, souls in Purgatory take on a human shape or appearance and return to Earth. For many Protestants, on the other hand, only demons masquerade as ghosts.[5] In short, the dramatic use of ghosts is closely related to the essence of the tragic vision: revenge, belief, representation, *hubris*, *hamartia*, denouement and death.

Chapter Seven
The New Regime, The Problem Plays

The final years of the sixteenth century and the first decade of the new century are not only those of Shakespeare's remarkable outpouring of great tragedies. To them belong other work, including the 'problem plays' or 'bitter comedies' such as *All's Well That End's Well*, *Troilus and Cressida* and *Measure for Measure*, in addition to more obvious collaborations such as, for instance, *Pericles* and other work. Before turning to these, it is best to go over the political and social events of these years and what is known personally regarding Shakespeare's life using contemporary documentary records.

The Turn of the Century

The turn of the century and the early years of the new one witnessed great political and social uncertainty. There was regime change and rebellion, and the situation in Ireland and on the European continent was chaotic. Further afield, England and Spain were fighting for rich pickings across the Atlantic Ocean and in the Caribbean. These conflicts are represented on a yearly basis.

1601

The year 1601 saw the summoning of Queen Elizabeth's thirteenth parliament, Essex' rebellion, trial and execution. On the coast opposite England, Ostend was under siege, and a Spanish attack on Ireland was repulsed. Domestically, a New Poor Law was passed that threw responsibility on the parish and local authorities for the poor and remained on the statute books basically unchanged until 1834. The year also witnessed the death of Shakespeare's father, John, who was buried on 8 September. In the London theatrical world, a conflict between dramatists such as Ben Jonson against John Marston and Thomas Dekker was at its height, with the former hurling abuse at the other two and vice versa.

1602

The following year, 1602, witnessed the exposure of plots against the life of the French monarch, Henry IV (1553–1610), and a proclamation expelling the Jesuits and secular priests from England. A landmark voyage by Bartholomew Gosnold (1572–1607) opened up settlement possibilities in the New World.

It was also an important year in Shakespeare's life, revealing his prosperity. The deed of conveyance whereby on 1 May 1602 he purchased 107 acres of land in the Stratford-upon-Avon parish was auctioned at Sotheby's in London on 11 December 1997. Shakespeare obtained from William Combe (d. 1667) and his uncle John Combe (d. 1614), members of a very wealthy land-owning family in and around Stratford, the acres consisting of open fields to the north of Old Stratford for the relatively large amount of £320.

This transaction testifies to Shakespeare's second major investment in his home town of Stratford. In 1597, he had purchased New Place, which was then perhaps the largest house in Stratford, from the recusant William Underhill (1557–1597). Further, on 28 September 1602, Shakespeare purchased from Walter Getley a nearby piece of land and cottage on Chapel Lane. In 1605, he purchased from Ralph Huband a substantial share in the Stratford tithes. These investments were, of course, in addition to his ownership of the 'Birthplace' house which Shakespeare inherited in 1601 when his father died.

It is perhaps not coincidental that the years during which Shakespeare made these investments witnessed disruption and uncertainty in Stratford, including two 'disastrous fires' in 1594 and 1595. These destroyed upwards of 200 buildings in the centre of the town and placed at least 400 people on poor relief. There were sequences of bad harvests and corn shortages and inflation. By 1601, about 700 people, roughly one-third of the total population of the town, were 'registered as paupers'. Consequently, there was a fear of rebellion. Shakespeare invested in his local town during this period of crisis, representing confidence in its future and also probably purchasing at cheaper prices than if the times had been less uncertain. He seems not to have returned to Stratford to sign the transfer deed for the land purchase. His brother, Gilbert, represented him.[6]

1603

On 24 March 1603, Elizabeth I died. Her funeral took place on 28 April 1603. James VI of Scotland, Elizabeth's choice as her successor, came to the throne as James I. It was indeed a year of transformation. In Ireland, the rebellious Hugh O'Neill, 2nd Earl of Tyrone finally surrendered. On the mainland, heralding religious conflicts to come, the Millenary Petition represented Puritan demands for reformation within the Anglican Church, and an Act of Uniformity, or conformity to the Church of England, was reinforced. At least one plot to overthrow James, the Cobham Plot, was uncovered. In this instance, Sir Walter Raleigh was implicated and imprisoned. In 1618 he was executed. James I, in order to raise needed revenues, started to sell knighthoods, indicative of court corruption. Overseas, in the New World, the explorer Bartholomew Gilbert (d. 1603) voyaged to Virginia, once again demonstrating the potential of a 'brave new world' (*The Tempest* 5. 1. 184). In the meantime, London was ravaged by the plague with over 30,500 recorded deaths.

In the theatrical world, Shakespeare was recorded as one of the 'principall Tragoedians' in the list of actors for Ben Jonson's satirical exposure of a deeply corrupt political world, *Sejanus* (performed 1603). Indeed, Jonson was summoned by the Privy Council and had to respond to accusations of treason. The appearance of Shakespeare's name serves as a salutary reminder not merely of his success, but of the fact that he was an exceedingly accomplished actor, rumoured to have performed as the gravedigger in *Hamlet*.

On 17 May 1603, there was a royal warrant licensing the Chamberlain's Men (Shakespeare's Company) as the King's Men.

During the second half of the year, and until April 1604 owing to the plague, the London theatres were closed. This has led to speculation that Shakespeare possibly may have visited Lady Pembroke (1561–1621), the third wife of the 2nd Earl of Pembroke (?1534–1601), sister of the poet, courtier and soldier Philip Sidney (1554–1586) and a patron of Ben Jonson. She lived at Wilton House in Wiltshire where, between October and December 1602, *As You Like It* was performed for the King.

1604

This, too, was a turbulent year. This was the year of the Hampton Court Conference, which was an attempt to paper over the fissures in the Protestant community and to herald a new translation of the Bible. It appointed a 47 strong committee to prepare what became the great King James or Authorized version of the Bible, published in 1611. This provided wonderful illustrations of Elizabethan and Jacobean poetry and prose at its finest. But it was not the Bible drawn upon by Shakespeare, whose work shows the influence of the Geneva Bible of 1560 and the 1568 Bishops' Bible (see Dobson and Wells: 45 and Shaheen).

All was not well in James's England. A proclamation banned Jesuits and seminary priests. Revenge was vowed, leading in the following year to the abortive Gun Powder Plot to blow up the Houses of Parliament. James's initial parliament asserted electoral rights and the freedom of members from arrest. Witchcraft, flourishing in times of uncertainty, had severe penalties imposed upon it. The long serving Archbishop of Canterbury, John Whitgift (b. *c.*1530), died at the end of February 1604. He was replaced by Richard Bancroft (1544–1610), whose Archbishopric was far shorter. Bancroft is largely remembered for being the chief architect of the 1611 Authorized Version of the Bible and his unsympathetic tolerance of zealots.

Although a peace treaty was made with England's chief external enemy, Spain, the Spanish occupied Ostend – an economic and strategic area crucial to English interests. Further afield, there were voyages to New England and an attempt to establish a colony in Guiana.

At home, an attempt was made to restrict tobacco usage by imposing a special tax on the commodity.

As for Shakespeare, on 1 January 1604, 'A play of Robin goode-fellow', most likely *A Midsummer Night's Dream*, was performed at Court. On 1 November 1604, 'The Moor of Venice' was performed at Whitehall, as were 'A play of the Merry Wives of Winsor' on 4 November. The day after Christmas, 1604, 'A play Caled Mesur for Mesur' was also performed, probably before the monarch at Whitehall. Another marker of Shakespeare's success is seen in his being granted, as a member of the King's Men, four yards of red cloth to mark the new King's regal procession through London on 15 March 1604 (*Riverside*: 2008).

Shakespeare as Lodger

One of the most interesting discoveries of the past century or so in the factual documentation of Shakespeare's life is that of his residency as a lodger, probably between 1603–1604 and 1612, in Silver Street in Cripplegate, London, with the Mountjoy family. The house he lived in was most probably burnt down in the Great Fire of 1666; the whole area was destroyed during the German Air Raid of 29 December 1940. Shakespeare's connection with the Mountjoys, a Huguenot family, was initially uncovered very early on in the twentieth century. In 1909, two American scholars, Charles Wallace (1865–1932) and his wife Hulda, from the University of Nebraska, discovered records of Shakespeare's deposition at what was then the Record Office, Chancery Lane. This was part of an attempt by a Stephen Belott (d. ?1646) 'to extract a marriage settlement from his father-in-law, a Huguenot Christopher Mountjoy [d. ?1620], Shakespeare's former landlord' (Katherine Duncan-Jones: 25).

This discovery forms the basis for a monograph published in 2007 by Charles Nicoll entitled *The Lodger: Shakespeare on Silver Street* (in America entitled *The Lodger Shakespeare: His Life on Silver Street*). Nicoll draws attention to allusions to the silk-weaving in which the Mountjoys were chiefly employed in, for instance, Macbeth's 'Sleep that knits up the ravell'd sleave of care' (2. 2. 34). Nicoll notes that

'Sleep brings order to this bundle of emotions as the hand of a silk-worker unravels a tangled sheaf of sleeve-silk', as opposed to the sense 'that the anxious mind is repaired by sleep, as a frayed sleeve is required by knitting' (American edition: 166). Also interestingly, Nicoll observes that a neighbour of the Mountjoys was William Tailer, or Tailor, an embroiderer. He writes, 'on 1 December 1605 a daughter of Tailor's was baptized at St. Olave's [the nearby parish church]. She was christened Cordelia. The name . . . was still unusual and was more often found in the Celtic form, Cordula (or Cordell)' (70). And, of course, Mountjoy is the surname of the French herald found in *Henry V*.

This is returning to the world of speculation that Shakespearean biography is so prone to. All that can definitely be said is that, thanks to the discoveries of the Wallaces (Wallace subsequently struck it rich again with oil wells in Texas [Schoenbaum: 464–472]), we know that Shakespeare did reside in Silver Street with the Mountjoys during the first decade of the seventeenth century and did give evidence during the Belott-Mountjoy 1612 marital settlement dispute. We also know that the Mountjoys were involved in the fashion business and that Shakespeare's landlady was French. Further, the deposition has Shakespeare's signature. 'For once the hand is not cramped by the small space available on the labels of conveyancing documents, or quavering from mortal illness, as when he revised his will.' It was used to demonstrate 'that the three pages of Addition D in the (co-authored) manuscript play of *Sir Thomas More*' are assigned to the first decade of the seventeenth century and that the pages 'are in Shakespeare's autograph' (Schoenbaum: 467).

1605

In the following year, on 24 July 1605, Shakespeare obtained tithes in Stratford. Further, he was left on 4 May 'a thirty shillings peece in gold' in the will of Augustine Phillips (d. 1605), a fellow actor in the Strange's Men and subsequently the Chamberlain's Men. Between 1 and 6 January, 1605, 'a play of "Loves Labours Lost"' was performed at Whitehall, on 7 January *Henry V* and on 10 and 12 February *The Merchant of Venice*.

On the national political domestic front, in addition to the Gun Powder Plot of 5 November, the King urged stronger action against Catholics and dissident Puritans. A daughter, Mary, was born to James and, in order to attempt to quiet down the turbulent Irish situation, on 11 March an amnesty was granted to the Irish rebels. On the theatrical front, new theatres such as the Red Bull at St. James Clerkenwell were built under the patronage of Queen Anne (1574–1619), the wife of James I, and utilized by the King's Men until 1617. The *Act to Restrain Abuses of Players* against profanity and attacks on the establishment was passed in 1606 (*Riverside*: 2010).

1606

This year also witnessed the London and Plymouth companies receiving charters allowing the colonization of Virginia. On the parliamentary and political fronts, a proposed union of England and Scotland was rebutted, an Oath of Allegiance enforced and a leading Jesuit executed as a collaborator in the Gun Powder Plot. There was considerable concern over the Jesuit doctrine of equivocation. Some of this is probably represented in the third scene of the second act of *Macbeth* (2. 3. 8–9). Heavy fines, too, were levied for failure to attend Anglican services and to receive the sacrament.

1607

In the emerging colonies, a plantation expedition sailed on 19 December 1606 to Virginia, and the following year in Jamestown, Virginia, a colony was established: it did not last very long. At home, 1607 witnessed disputes between the ecclesiastical courts and the civil ones. The latter gained a powerful voice with the appointment of the erudite, well-connected Francis Bacon (1561–1627) as Solicitor-General.

Important personal events took place in Shakespeare's life. On 5 June 1607, Susanna, his daughter, married the physician John Hall, in Stratford. Edmund, Shakespeare's brother, died and was buried on 5 September 1607.

1608

The year 1608 witnessed the birth of Elizabeth Hall, Shakespeare's granddaughter, who was christened on 21 February. She died as Shakespeare's last remaining direct descendant in 1670. Shakespeare's mother, Mary, was buried on 9 September. Slightly earlier, Shakespeare sued a Stratford gentleman for debt. The case dragged on from 17 December until 7 June 1609. Eventually, a jury awarded Shakespeare his debt and the costs.

In the theatrical world, Shakespeare became a one-seventh shareholder in the second Blackfriars Theatre. This was leased in 1608 by the King's Men from the actor Richard Burbage as a private rather than a public theatre. The King's Men began performing in the theatre in the autumn of 1609 and continued to perform there until 1642 and the outbreak of the Civil War.

1609

In 1609, a Quarto version of Shakespeare's Sonnets appeared, printed by 'TT' – assumed to be the printer Thomas Thorpe and enigmatically dedicated to 'Mr. W. H.' The identity of 'Mr. W. H.' has been the subject of much speculation. As Stanley Wells observes: 'If Thorpe's use of initials was intended to conceal the truth from all but a select band of readers in his own time, he must be considered wholly successful' (Dobson and Wells: 306).

Politically, the struggle over the authority of the monarch is reflected in the attempt to prevent James removing a case from the civil jurisdiction to the ecclesiastical courts. On the European continent, what became known as the Thirty Years War was brewing with the formation by Maximilian (1573–1651), the Duke of Bavaria, of a Catholic Defence League. The Moors were once again expelled from Spain. Further afield, the Bermudas were claimed for the English monarchy by the Virginia Company and in 1612, colonized with settlements.

On the theatrical front, and not confined to the year 1609 alone, the London theatres were very active, with dramas by Francis Beaumont (1584/5–1616) and John Fletcher (1579–1625), Cyril

Tourneur (d. 1626) and Thomas Middleton, working sometimes in collaboration. In 1609, Jonson's *The Masque of Queens* was the first recorded to exploit the anti-masque device. The masque form, in fact a highly developed kind of court entertainment, amalgamated poetic drama, music, ballet, elaborate costumes and tremendous stage spectacle. Elements of *The Tempest* provide a wonderful example of this. Jonson's anti-masque form focused upon anarchic characters, ridiculous action and frequently very coarse humour as a counterpart to the order, ceremony and elegant structures of the masque form. Shakespeare probably did not live long enough to fully exploit the form.

1610

The final year of the decade contains a record of Shakespeare holding a lease on a Henley Street, Stratford barn he probably inherited from his father. Many biographers speculate that this is the year in which Shakespeare is supposed to have returned home to Stratford. Contemporary records reveal that on 30 April 1610, *Othello* was performed at the Globe, *Pericles* and *King Lear*, too, saw performances in Yorkshire.

The year also witnessed Parliament issuing a Petition of Grievances and a Petition of Right as witnesses to its dissatisfaction with James I's reign. James, in return, in February 1611 dissolved his initial parliament in anger. His eldest son, Henry, was created Prince of Wales. On the European Continent, Henry IV of France (b. 1553) associated himself with the Protestant cause and was assassinated.

Problem Plays

Such then is an outline of selected political, theatrical and personal happenings during the years witnessing the summit of Shakespeare's great creativity represented by the tragedies and also by a group of complex, not easily categorized plays, called the 'Problem Plays' or 'Bitter Comedies'. They were described in this manner by the important Belfast-born scholar Frederick Samuel Boas (1862–1957) in

Shakespeare and his Predecessors (1896). Boas, from 1905 to 1927, worked as a school inspector in London and from 1922 until 1955 served as editor of *The Year's Work in English Studies*, a time probably remaining unequalled. He applied the terms to *Hamlet, All's Well That Ends Well, Troilus and Cressida* and *Measure for Measure*. According to W. W. Lawrence in his *Shakespeare's Problem Comedies* (1931), these plays (excluding *Hamlet*) 'clearly do not fall into the category of tragedy, and yet are too serious and analytic to fit the commonly accepted conception of comedy' (cited Dobson and Wells: 357).

Measure for Measure

Central to the problem plays is the exploration of ignoble areas of human behaviour. Nothing really is solved except perhaps in the most superficial manner concerning the issues, largely moral ones, presented in the drama. For instance, in the lengthy final act of *Measure for Measure*, the Duke seems to resolve areas of conflict in the play. Mariana is given the choice of widowhood and rather surprisingly pleads for Angelo's life. She tells an incredulous Duke, 'O my dear lord, | I crave no other, nor no better man' than Angelo (5. 1. 425–426), and asks a somewhat reluctant Isabella to also plead for Angelo. The only one who seems to be punished is the rebellious Lucio, who previously insulted the Duke, claiming to be familiar with him. As Lucio says in his final words, 'Marrying a punk [prostitute, also with the implications of rotten and mouldy], my lord, is pressing to death, whipping, and hanging', to which the Duke replies, 'Slandering a prince deserves it.' In his final speech, the Duke addresses Isabel: 'Dear Isabel . . . What's mine is yours, and what is yours is mine' (5. 1. 522–524, 534, 537). In some productions, they leave the stage hand in hand; in others, they separately leave the stage. There is no verbal indication or stage direction that Isabel actually agrees to what the Duke proposes or doesn't agree.

Other features of the problem plays are not only the unresolved, ambiguous conclusions. In them there is an intermingling of people of high degree, of the nobility and of the very lowest classes, of not only the Monarch, Kings, Dukes and the aristocracy with prostitutes, pimps, the brothel workers. Lucio 'a fantastic', according to the dramatis personae, bridges these worlds. He mixes with the highest and the lowest. He claims to be intimately acquainted with the highest in Vienna, with 'the old fantastical Duke of dark corners' (4. 3. 156–157), yet is very familiar with Pompey, Froth and Mistress Overdone from the world of the brothels.

Further, there is another pattern in the problem plays. They depict a serious action that heralded a tragic conclusion to a protagonist such as Claudio; however, there is a sudden, abrupt change of circumstances, so that the conclusion doesn't end in death but apparently happily. The Duke in *Measure for Measure* comes up with a substitute head and Claudio is saved. He lives, as does Angelo and of course Lucio.

Measure for Measure, *All's Well That Ends Well*, and *Troilus and Cressida* contain wonderful illustrations of Shakespeare's poetry at its finest, combined with some very indifferent lines. They contain an interesting synthesis of poetry and prose. Of the 2,671 lines in *Measure for Measure*, 59 per cent are in blank verse, 3.4 per cent in rhyme and 37.6 per cent in prose. There is one song, a very beautiful one, sung on behalf of the deserted Mariana:

> Take, O, take those lips away,
> That so sweetly were forsworn,
> And those eyes, the break of day,
> Lights that do mislead the morn;
> But my kisses bring again, bring again,
> Seals of love, but seal'd in vain, seal'd in vain (4. 1. 1–6).

The sad, melancholic tone, the implicit note of past sensuality and acknowledged false hope for repetition of what has occurred, are in accord with the modulation of erotic emotion conveyed in the play. Interestingly, some have attributed these lines to 'a late interpolation from [John] Fletcher's *Rollo, Duke of Normandy* (1616–[16]19)' (Dobson and Wells: 284).

The best lines are dispersed throughout the characters; they are by no means confined to the central protagonists. For instance, in the second scene of the drama, Mistress Overdone asks Pompey her servant 'what's his [Claudio's] offense?' He replies, 'Groping for trouts in a peculiar river' (1. 2. 89–90), a line brilliantly evoking the actual spawning behaviour of the trout. Earlier, in the same scene, prose is succinct, evocative and to the point. She confesses, 'what with the war, what with the sweat, what with the gallows, and what with poverty, I am custom-shrunk' (1. 2. 82–84). Disease, threats of execution, and the economic situation, has even affected the age-old trade of prostitution.

There are of course, many wonderful poetic moments in a play such as *Measure for Measure* that conform more to our expectations of Shakespearean poetry. Angelo, for instance, severely tormented by the sensual appeal Isabella has for him, expresses anguish and frustration in several powerful soliloquies: 'When I would pray and think, I think and pray | To several subjects.' He reveals:

> Heaven hath my empty words,
> Whilst my invention, hearing not my tongue,
> Anchors on Isabel (2. 4. 1–4).

Previously, following their initial encounter, after Isabel has left, Angelo asks himself a series of rhetorical questions:

> What's this, what's this? Is this her fault, or mine?
> The tempter or the tempted, who sins most, ha?
> Not she; nor doth she tempt; but it is I
> That, lying by the violet in the sun,
> Do, as the carrion does, not as the flow'r,
> Corrupt with virtuous season (2. 2. 162–167).

Natural imagery – that of flowers, of colour, of the sun, of birds of prey – combine to convey the anguished guilt-ridden, mental state.

These plays, too, are very difficult to interpret, as there is no consensus over their meaning or even stature in Shakespeare's oeuvre. There is agreement that a play such as *Measure for Measure* is preoccupied with philosophical issues, with power, and its nature, with disguise, hypocrisy, appearance and reality, and the nature of justice. The Duke tells Friar Thomas in the last lines of the third scene of the opening act: 'we shall see | If power change purpose: what our seemers be' (55). He seems to have relinquished his power to Angelo. The Duke is now disguised as a friar, waiting and observing in disguise the action as it unfolds; increasingly, he becomes aware that human beings, once they obtain power, are transformed.

On many levels, *Measure for Measure* explores the nature of 'justice', of 'law' and 'authority'. The play is also infused with religious allusions. Its very title, *Measure for Measure*, is taken from Jesus' *Sermon on the Mount*: 'Judge not, that ye be not judged. For with what judgment ye judge, ye shall be judged: and with what measure ye meet, it shall be measured to you again' (Mt. 7 1–2). There is a warning here: if you pass judgment, you, too, will be judged. Critics such as Roy W. Battenhouse, in his *'Measure for Measure* and the Doctrine of Atonement', argue that the Duke plays God, acting in disguise 'like pow'r divine' (5. 1. 369) as he observes in the background the unfolding actions of the play. He has initiated them by not enforcing the laws in the first place, and secondly by placing Angelo in office as a kind of test of Angelo's character. A problem is that the Duke is not as he seems, and to paraphrase Isabella's words, bids her to 'seek redemption of the devil', that is, Angelo (5. 1. 29). G. Wilson Knight (1897–1985), writing on *'Measure for Measure* and the Gospels' in his *The Wheel of Fire* (1930), viewed the play as a parable. For Wilson Knight, *Measure for Measure* is an explication of the theme 'Judge not, that ye be not judged', and the Duke is 'the prophet of an enlightened ethic' with Isabella as self-absorbed (81).

In one of the epigrammatic quips not uncommon to a drama preoccupied with philosophical, moral and religious concerns, the wise Escalus, who should have been given power rather than the task of observing Angelo as his Deputy, comments, 'Some rise by sin, and some by virtue fall' (2. 1. 38). In another of the marvellous lines containing insight into human character and events, Isabella pleads for mercy before Angelo, reminding him of human folly and vanity:

> but man, proud man,
> Dress'd in a little brief authority,
> Most ignorant of what he's most assur'd,
> His glassy [fragile, illusory] essence, like an angry ape
> Plays such fantastic tricks before high heaven
> As makes the angels weep, who, with our spleens [the spleen was

thought to be the seat of laughter],
Would all themselves laugh mortal.

The 'ape' (2. 2. 117–123) image is wonderfully apposite. Man is compared to his nearest physical counterpart in the animal kingdom. The human being in his illusory, transient, puffed up glory, is transformed into a creature of fantastic imitation.

It is no wonder that this play, with its theological subtexts, has puzzled the critics through the centuries. Samuel Johnson was perplexed by its complex moral aspects; and these aspects alienated the romantic poet and critic S. T. Coleridge (1772–1834). In the last years of the twentieth century, new historicist critics found in the text wisdom from the brothels and an apt social commentary on society from those who are marginalized, the pimps and the bawds, rather than from the Duke at the centre of authority. The exposure of hypocrisy and leadership, the hollow nature of power, reinforces such a perspective in a play that emphasizes seeming – what appears to be but isn't.

On the other hand, for a drama focusing on female exploitation and resistance to male authority, there have been surprisingly few feminist readings. These focus on sex and sexuality in a play that is not short of sexual imagery and innuendo. Readings have focused on Isabella, her role, attitudes and responses to the other characters. They examine the manner of her initial appearance in the play, the way she behaves during her interviews with Angelo, and in the unresolved, ambiguous final act. She does function as other women in the play, signifying woman's availability to men. Mistress Overdone is available to males as a commodity, depends upon them for her livelihood and exploits them as much as they have exploited her. Juliet is guilty of fornication but acts out of her own accord. She is offered little comfort. She answers in the affirmative when the Duke, in his disguise as a Friar, asks 'Love you the man that wrong'd you?' The Duke responds, 'So then it seems your most offenseful act | Was mutually committed?' Juliet, then, replies, 'Mutually'. The Duke, still in disguised as the Friar, passes judgement: 'Then was your sin of heavier kind than his' (2. 3. 24, 26–28).

In order to make her own marriage to Angelo legal, Mariana functions as a surrogate for Isabella in the bed trick. Almost ignored, probably due to the prevailing mores in Western European and North American educated circles, is the issue of the value of virginity raised in the play. For her virginity, Isabella literally is willing to sacrifice the life of her brother. She visits the condemned Claudio in prison the day before his planned execution. She tells him:

> Dost thou think, Claudio,
> If I would yield him my virginity,
> Thou mightst be freed!

She hardly gives Claudio the opportunity to respond by sanctimoniously telling him,

> O, were it but my life,
> I'd throw it down for your deliverance
> As frankly [freely] as a pin (3. 1. 96–98, 104–106).[7]

Of course, she may have seen through Angelo's bluff: even if she'd slept with him, he may well have not kept his word and still ordered the execution of her brother.

Textually, *Measure for Measure* is not complicated. It is found in the 1623 *First Folio*. Modern scholarship has detected some collaborative hands, such as those of Fletcher and Middleton, at work in small portions of the play. For example, in the beautiful 'Take, O take those lips away' song at the start of the fourth act and in the Duke's all too brief soliloquy in the same scene, beginning, 'O place and greatness! millions of false eyes | Are stuck upon thee' (1, 59–60: see Dobson and Wells: 284, and Taylor and Lavagnino: 681–682).

The first recorded performance of *Measure for Measure* is that in the Revels accounts (i.e. the accounts of the court entertainments), which notes a court performance on 26 December 1604 (*Riverside*: 2008). It was subsequently revived after the Restoration in adaptations by William Davenant (1606–1668), who, according to rumour, was Shakespeare's illegitimate son, and by the dramatist Charles Gildon (1665–1724). At the start of the second decade of the eighteenth century, Shakespeare's text was restored to the stage. It was then largely ignored until more frequent performances during the second half of the twentieth century.

There are contemporary allusions in the play that help to date it. In the opening lines of the second scene, Lucio tells two Gentlemen: 'If the Duke with other dukes comes not to composition [agreement] with the King of Hungary, why then all the dukes fall upon [attack] the King.' The first Gentleman responds, 'Heaven grant us its peace, but not the King of Hungary's!' (1–4). Unless this is a subsequent interpolation introduced into the *First Folio* text, then this is a very contemporary reference to the peace agreement signed by King James I with Spain at Hampton Court on 18 August 1604. Also, the Duke of Holst, the brother of Queen Anne – James's wife – was active in London in the winter of 1604, attempting to raise an army to defend the new Protestant ruler of Hungary. On 16 September 1603, King James took action against the proliferating brothel houses of the London suburbs. This action may well underlie the chat between Mistress Overdone and Pompey in the same scene. Mistress Overdone asks him, 'What proclamation man?' Pompey replies, 'All houses in the suburbs [outside of the city walls] of Vienna must be pluck'd down' (95–96).

All's Well That Ends Well

A bed-trick, the substitution of one for another, also takes place in another problem play, *All's Well That Ends Well*. In this drama, Helena, the orphan daughter of a physician, is so obsessed with Bertram, son of the widowed Countess of Roussillon, that she is prepared to suffer almost any indignity to marry and to consummate their marriage, including pretending to be someone else in order to have sexual relations with him. Sexual desire and consummation in the play appear to be built upon frustration and inaccessibility. The play, too, is replete with contradictions. For instance, in the fourth scene of the second act, Helena asks the Countess's misanthropic servant, Lavache, if the Countess is well. Lavache responds to the question, 'She is not well,' and then adds, 'but yet she has her health. She's very merry, but yet she is not well; but thanks be given, she's very well and wants nothing i' th' world; but yet she is not well' (1–4). For Lavache, only the dead can be happy, and he reflects a view that we live in an imperfect world where there is no happiness. In the third scene of the fourth act, the First Lord comments stoically, 'As we are our-selves, what things are we!' (19–20).

In common with *Measure for Measure*, the ending is ambiguous. Bertram in the final scene has to be rescued by his wife (Helena) from possible murder and other charges. His response is that of relief. Bertram tells the King, 'If she [Helena] my liege, can make me know this clearly | I'll love her dearly, ever, ever dearly' (314–315). In other words, that his love is part of what he owes his wife, what it costs him to be saved from the charges. Even the King at the end has his doubts: 'All yet seems well, and if it end so meet, | The bitter past, more welcome is the sweet.'

Measure for Measure, *Troilus and Cressida* and *All's Well That Ends Well* are also preoccupied with the implications of 'seems', a word that recurs at the end of *All's Well That Ends Well* (5. 3. 333–334) and refers to what appears to be so as opposed to what actually is so. The seemingly well-educated and well-bred Bertram behaves without honour or ethics. In *Troilus and Cressida*, Achilles, a classical hero, is a murderer. Parolles, Bertram's companion, reveals himself to be a coward. The apparently virtuous Angelo in *Measure for Measure* exposes himself as a hypocrite and a liar who exploits the power he is given for corrupt purposes.

There do not appear to be too many textual problems involving *All's Well That Ends Well*. The play's first printed appearance is in the *First Folio* of 1623. There are some interesting features, such as the play's clear division into five acts. The use of cornets indicated in the stage directions is interesting as cornets usually replace trum-pets in indoor theatrical performances whereas trumpets were mainly used in open air theatres. In the *First Folio*, the initials 'G' and 'E' are used as speech prefixes for the Dumaine brothers. 'G' may well stand for Robert Gough (d. 1624), an actor for the King's Men. 'E' may well refer to William Ecclestone (*c*.1591–post 1623), who acted for the King's Men between 1610 and 1611, and from 1614 to 1623. Given the thematic and verbal similarities, the play is usually dated alongside *Measure for Measure* and *Troilus and Cressida* and assigned to 1604 to 1605.

The performance history of the play resembles its critical fortunes. The first recorded performance was not until 1741. During that dec-ade, it was popular but subsequently performed infrequently. In the twentieth century, considerable textual liberties were taken with it. For instance, a production in 1920 by William Poel (1850–1934) depicted Helena as a suffragette. Tyrone Guthrie's (1900–1971) 1959 production left out Lavache, truncated the text, used an Edwardian setting, and presented the war scenes in a comic manner. Sir Peter Hall's (1930–) 1992 Royal Shakespeare Company production followed the text more literally and played the drama more or less straight.

Critically, until the last years of the twentieth century, not a good deal of attention was paid to *All's Well That Ends Well*. Shakespeare's use of his sources, folk tales, discussion of the unity or not of the play, defence of Bertram's character, the morality expressed in the third scene of the fourth act in 'The web of our life is of a mingled yarn, good and ill together' (71–72), Parolles's character, adaptability, whatever the circumstances, provided he survives, and the affinities with other problem plays, attracted attention. Recently, critical focus has also been paid to the representation of the women in *All's Well That End's Well* and in the other Shakespearean plays.[8]

Troilus and Cressida

Unlike *All's Well That End's Well* or *Measure for Measure*, *Troilus and Cressida* has a complex textual history, somewhat akin to its performance and interpretative history. The play is found entered in the Stationers' Register for 7 February 1603 by James Roberts. Roberts published several Shakespeare Quartos, held a monopoly on printing playbills, and was closely associated with the Lord Chamberlain's Men. *Troilus and Cressida* was not published in 1603 and Roberts may well have been engaged in a blocking action in order to stop others pirating the play and illegally performing it.

The play was published in 1609 in two different Quarto editions, published by Richard Bonian and Henry Walley, about whom little is known. The printer was George Eld (fl. 1603–1624) who printed 34 play quartos, including Shakespeare's Sonnets in 1609. The Quartos have a different title page and there is an added 'Epistle' prior to the first scene of the first act. One of the Quartos claims that it prints the play as it was 'acted by the King's Majesty's servants at the Globe'. The other omits this: its title contains a wonderful expression announcing 'a new play, never stal'd with the stage, never clapper-claw'd with the palms of the vulgar' (*Riverside*: 477).

Such differences have led to much speculation concerning the early history of *Troilus and Cressida*. Speculation ranges from the theories that the play was written to be privately performed, and the theory that its performance was censored as the character of Achilles reflected too well the character of the Earl of Essex, executed for treason in 1601. On the other hand, the title page of the second 1609 Quarto could contain genuine error, deliberately exaggerated in order to attract interest in performances of *Troilus and Cressida* or reflecting snobbery. The play did get into the 1623 *First Folio*, its text being based on the Q texts with many minor variations. It also adds a 'Prologue' and another forty or so smaller passages not present in the early texts. Also, it is probable that the play was a late addition to the *First Folio*, as it is omitted from the table of contents or 'Catalogue' and placed between the final play of the histories, *All Is True* (*Henry VIII*), and *Coriolanus* – supposedly the first of the tragedies. The Quarto and Folio texts lack act or scene divisions, although the first scene in the latter is named '*Actus Primus. Scoena Prima*'. The actual scene divisions were added early in the eighteenth century.

Again, dating is unclear. Published in 1609, it is noted in the Stationers' Register in February 1603. Roberts' entry partly reads 'The booke of Troilus and Cressida as yt is acted by my lo: Chamberlens Men'. It is consequently assumed that some kind of text existed prior to February 1603. However, there is no record of a production in England until 1907! There was a Munich production in German in 1898. In 1679, John Dryden produced the abridged *Troilus and Cressida [or] Truth Found Too Late*. In this, Cressida remains faithful and dies, as do Troilus and Diomedes. The play's relativism, its contrasts between medieval, or chivalric codes of honour and Greek cynicism, the lack of fixity, of rootlessness, and its depiction of complex sexuality, have appealed to the last and present century and resulted in fascinating, diverse productions.[9]

The late A. D. Nuttall (1937–2007) shrewdly observes in his *Shakespeare the Thinker* (2007): '*Troilus and Cressida* is about the sadness of broken faith in a world of hollow men'. For Nuttall, it is also 'a philosophical play and it deals with the foundation of ethical judgements'. Nuttall distinguishes it from, for instance, *The Merchant of Venice* or *Measure for Measure*, plays 'about the application of ethical principles. Each play interrogates the standard notion "Mercy is higher than justice"' (255).

Characteristics of the Problem Plays

Troilus and Cressida has much in common thematically and dramatically, in terms of character, treatment of gender, language and tone, with the other problem plays, *Measure for Measure* and *All's Well That Ends Well*. Let's enumerate these:

- Not all of the central characters die at the end of *Troilus and Cressida*, so it is not a tragedy. In common with the other problem plays, it is not a comedy, either. The conclusion of all three is decidedly ambivalent. At the end of the play, Troilus looks forward to revenge: 'To Troy with comfort [this reassurance] go; | Hope of revenge shall hide our inward woe.' In the last lines, as he exits, Pandarus cynically says to the audience, 'And at that [this] time bequeath you my diseases' (5. 10. 30–31, 55).
- The three dramas contain in almost the same position a key debate scene. In the second scene of the second act of *Troilus and Cressida*, King Priam and his sons Hector, Troilus, Paris and Helenus consider whether it is worth continuing fighting. The debate intensifies after the appearance of their sister, Cassandra. She prophesizes that Troy will be destroyed unless Helen is returned to the Greeks. So questions of honour, value and worth, among others, are being debated. Similarly, in the third scene of the second act of *All's Well That Ends Well*, the nature, value, consequences and implications of human choice are discussed. Law, justice, abuse and the limitations of power are the subjects in the second scene of act two of *Measure for Measure*, although, of course, they permeate the whole drama.
- The three plays investigate the nature of the interaction between our human behaviour, the ways in which we conduct ourselves, and the institutions to which we belong or pledge allegiance. These plays reverberate with questions concerning authority, the ways

in which decisions are made and the consequences of these decisions for the individual and society in general. For instance, how far can a ruler go, and how far can law restrain natural human behaviour? Pompey rhetorically asks Escalus in the first scene of the second act of *Measure for Measure,* after he has learnt that the laws against brothels are being strongly enforced, 'Does your worship mean to geld and splay all the youth of the city?' (231).

- Fourthly, as has been noted, all three plays, in common with other Shakespearean plays, are very much concerned with 'seeming', with the relationship with what appears to be so and what actually is so.

- Fifthly, the three plays contain characters who seem to be unsympathetic, nuisances, thorns in the flesh of authority, and who will not submit to authority. Pandarus in *Troilus and Cressida* is comic, satirical and hyperbolical. Thersites, in *Troilus and Cressida*, rails, contradicts, is inconsistent and self-hating: 'I am a rascal, a scurvy railing knave, a very filthy rogue' (5. 4. 28), and again 'I am a bastard too, I love bastards. I am bastard begot, bastard instructed, bastard in mind, bastard in valor, in every thing illegitimate' (5. 7. 16–18). In *Measure for Measure*, Lucio is a self-proclaimed 'kind of bur, I shall stick' (4. 3. 179). Seemingly unafraid to libel the Duke, he encourages Isabella not to give up pleading on her brother's behalf. In *All's Well That Ends Well,* Parolles, appropriately named after the French for 'words' or hot air, pretends to be heroic and a big fighter. He, too, in Helena's words, is 'a notorious liar' and 'a great way fool, soly a coward' (1. 1. 100–101), and, according to the Countess, a 'very tainted fellow, and full of wickedness' (3. 2. 87). A great survivor of the vicissitudes of human existence, for Parolles, 'Simply the thing I am | Shall make me live . . . | There's place and means for every man alive' (4. 3. 333–334; 339). In common with Lucio, Thersites and Parolles are liars, yet represent those who refuse to conform to dictators. They represent defiance and attack anyone in a position of authority who takes themselves too seriously.

- All three plays, reminiscent of Falstaff in *Henry IV Part 1*, investigate the concept of honour. Isabella in *Measure for Measure* is prepared to sacrifice her brother for what she perceives to be the honour of maintaining her virginity. Confronted by the sexual power and attraction of Isabella, Angelo is prepared to renounce all idea of honour. Hector in *Troilus and Cressida*, too, is obsessed with honour, 'the faith of valor' (5. 3. 68), placing it above even life itself. He ignores the pleading of his wife and father. The Countess's love for her son, Bertram, in *All's Well That Ends Well* is not enough to excuse his behaviour. She recognizes that he is a 'rash and unbridled boy' (3. 2. 27). In her mind, even his battle-field heroics cannot excuse him.

• Sex is a dominant concern of these problem plays. The Trojan Wars are fought over a sexual obsession and the lack of fidelity. Helen and Cressida are objects of desire and emblems of human folly. Angelo is prepared to risk all for sexual gratification and, at the same time, he condemns Claudio to execution for sleeping consensually with the woman he is engaged to and loves. Sex as a commercial commodity resists all attempts to curb it. Bertram in *All's Well That Ends Well* has no scruples about seduction, dishonour and falsely denounces the woman he seduced as a prostitute. Frustration and desire, on the individual level, social and institutional attempts at restraint are key components of these dramas. They continue the conflict represented in *Twelfth Night* between Sir Toby Belch's hedonism and Malvolio's hypocritical Puritanism and repression.

Finally, there is a disillusionment at the core of these plays. It is as if ideals are ultimately revealed to be limited and all too prone to human frailty. Helena in *All's Well That Ends Well* and Mariana in *Measure for Measure*, seemingly characters of high ideals, are attracted by unworthy characters such as Bertram and Angelo. In *Troilus and Cressida*, little of value is left, if anything as its Prologue asserts, 'Like or find fault, do as your [the audience's] pleasures are, | Now good or bad, 'tis but the chance of war' (30–31).

Conclusion

The three plays are replete with sexual imagery, ambiguity, a tendency to abstraction at times juxtaposed with specific imagery, the language of nature, lists of diseases and a very detailed knowledge of the processes of nature. In the opening scene of the final act of *Troilus and Cressida*, Thersites heaps curses on Patroclus: 'the rotten diseases of the south [probably Naples], the guts-griping, ruptures, catarrhs, loads o'gravel i' the back [kidney stones], lethargies [comatose states], cold palsies, raw eyes, dirt-rotten livers, whissing lungs, bladders full of imposthume [abscesses], sciaticas, lime-kills i' th' palm, incurable bone-ache.' The list intensifies: 'and the rivell'd fee-simple of the tetter [a skin disease characterized by eruptions and itching], take and take again such preposterous discoveries!' (17–22). Angelo in his soliloquy at the end of the second scene of the second act of *Measure for Measure* recognizes that he has succumbed to Isabella's temptation:

> it is I
> That, lying by the violet in the sun,
> Do as the carrion does, not as the flow'r
> Corrupt with virtuous season (164–167).

There is here knowledge that flowers rot in fine weather and, that, to quote the final line of Shakespeare's Sonnet 94, 'Lilies that fester smell far worse than weeds.'

There is indeed something cankered, disillusioned about these plays. Shakespeare's great tragic period, his most fertile creative period in which these problem plays are also the product, contains a vision of decay, of cynicism, of garbage and rotting vegetation. Whether this reflects something in his personal life or his perspective on the shifting social and political kaleidoscope of the opening years of the seventeenth century remains an enigma.

Chapter Eight
Shakespeare as Collaborator

The use of image patterns, analysing the sequence of three to seven words recurring in different texts written by the same author, the resources of computer generated/stylometric analysis and the results of authorial attribution studies, indicates that at least five Shakespeare works are considered to be collaborative. These works encompass chronologically the whole range of Shakespeare's creative work span. They include *Titus Andronicus*, regarded as his earliest tragedy, *Timon of Athens* from the period of the great tragedies, *Pericles*, one of the late romances, the very late – perhaps even post *The Tempest* – *All is True* (*Henry VIII*), and also the very late *The Two Noble Kinsmen*, which was excluded from the *First Folio*. The first part of Brian Vickers' important book Shakespeare, *Co-Author: A Historical Study of Five Collaborative Plays* (2002) discusses the standard processes of collaboration as they can be reconstructed from the plays themselves and from documents connected with the Elizabethan stage, such as the surviving correspondence and other dealings between the impresario Philip Henslowe and the group of script-writers to whom he fed sums of money in return for acts of a play (viii).

Henslowe's methods are brilliantly, imaginatively recreated in Marc Norman and Tom Stoppard's *Shakespeare in Love: A Screenplay* (1998) with his repeated, insistent demands upon his jobbing offers to produce, to deliver the goods. Henslowe is ever mindful of the competition. The first glimpse of him in *Shakespeare in Love* is as a 'man screaming . . . Desperately", he says to Shakespeare, 'Will! Where is my play? Tell me you have it nearly done!' (1, 5).

Sir Thomas More: *Shakespeare's Handwriting*

Vickers convincingly demonstrates 'that collaboration was very common in the Elizabethan, Jacobean and Caroline theatre, and that every major and most minor dramatists shared in the writing of plays.' Considerable attention is given to 'the only existing playhouse manuscript containing scenes written by Shakespeare', *Sir Thomas More*. Now at the British Library, the manuscript is in several hands: those of Anthony Munday (1560–1633), the copyist, and five others: Henry Chettle (*c*.1560–1607), Hand A; Thomas Heywood, probably Hand B; Thomas Dekker, Hand E; an unidentified playhouse scribe, Hand C; and Shakespeare, probably Hand D. There is a general consensus, although there are some sceptics, that three folios of the manuscript are 'more likely Shakespeare's autograph than not' (vii, 39).

The writing has curious characteristics. First, the amount of space used is uneconomical and expensive. The letter-forms are not necessarily larger than the others. 'The difference lies in the line-separation,' (Blayney cited in Vickers, *Shakespeare, Co-Author*: 39) as if Shakespeare 'were allowing himself ample space for interlinear additions and corrections'. There are spaces between words for punctuation marks to be subsequently added. The use of punctuation is thrifty. The conclusion of a sentence occurs 'in the middle of a line simply by leaving a wider space between its last word and the first word of the next sentence'. The spelling, too, appears to be that of Shakespeare. Utilizing the work of John Dover Wilson, and subsequently that of the South African scholar A. C. Partridge, it seems that Shakespeare's spelling habits are characterized by the omission of 'the *e* after *c* in words like "insolence" and "obedience"'. In addition, Shakespeare 'preferred the older spelling, with –*s* endings, rather than –*ss*.' Also, he omitted 'the mute terminal *e*, and' preferred 'the full vowel spellings for *shoold* and *woold*' (Vickers, *Shakespeare, Co-Author*: 39–41).[10]

P. J. Croft (1929–1984), Fellow and Librarian of King's College, Cambridge, in the first volume of his *Autograph Poetry and the English Language: Facsimiles of Original Manuscripts from the Fourteenth to the Twentieth Century* (1973) comments on the 'vigour and fluency' of Shakespeare's hand in the *More* example. For Croft, 'the general effect bears out the final tribute by Heminge[s] and Condell in the [*First Folio*]: "His mind and hand went together. And what he thought, he uttered with that easinesse, that wee have scarse received from him a blot in his papers"' (I: 23).

Handwriting and spelling are not the only means by which the *Sir Thomas More* lines have been attributed to Shakespeare for more than one hundred and fifty years. A consideration of imagery, dramatic style and rhetoric also contribute to the identification. The eminent New Zealand Shakespearean MacDonald P. Jackson, for instance, has demonstrated 'that Shakespeare's orthographical tendency was towards an increased use of the more colloquial forms' such as '*let's*', of which there are 5 instances; there are '4 of *we'll*, 3 of *th*', 2 of *you'll* and' single instances of '*has, by 'th*, to '*th, 'twere, what's, that's* and *there's*' (Vickers, *Shakespeare, Co-Author*: 88–89). Jackson writes, 'This gives a total of 21 such forms in 147 lines, or one for every 7 lines, a ratio of occurrence which unequivocally associates Hand D of *Sir Thomas More* with the post-1600 Shakespeare plays' (Jackson, 'Hand D of *Sir Thomas More*,' *Notes and Queries* 226 (1981) 146). Further 'parallels of language, especially thematic imagery, indirectly helped to date Shakespeare's contribution to the late 1590s or early 1600s' (Vickers, *Shakespeare, Co-Author*: 128). These thematic parallels include the treatment of the mob found in *Richard II* (*c*.1595), *Troilus and Cressida* (*c*.1602) and *Coriolanus* (*c*.1608).

Metrical and vocabulary linking also serve to pinpoint the dating of Shakespeare's contribution as the early years of the new century. The distinguished twentieth-century Italian scholar Giorgio Melchiori notes in his 'Hand D in *Sir Thomas More*: An Essay in Misinterpretation', *Shakespeare Survey*, 38 (1985) distinct differences in the presentation of the rioters between Anthony Munday's and Shakespeare's contribution, known as Hand D. Melchiori writes that 'while Munday in the rest of the play [*Sir Thomas More*] presented the leaders of the rebellion as fairly substantial citizens, for D they seem to be thoughtless apprentices one and all, an indiscriminate mass led by a trouble-maker.' Melchiori refers to Shakespeare's 'careless treatment of Lincoln and company as a bunch of fools, in contrast with their painstaking individual characterization in the original draft' (109, 112).

Titus Andronicus

Vickers examines the arguments for and against Shakespeare's co-authorship in five plays. He utilizes 'verse tests', 'parallel passages', 'vocabulary', 'linguistic preferences', 'function words', 'statistics', 'stylometry', 'language change' and 'social class' (*Shakespeare, Co-Author*, viii–x). The first play to be considered is the gruesome *Titus Andronicus*, in which body parts, rape and mutilation predominate. The play was entered in the Stationers' Register on 6 February 1594, described as 'a book intituled a Noble Roman Historye of Tytus Andronicus'. The First Quarto, published in 1594, describes it as 'The Most Lamentable Romaine Tragedie of Titus Andronicus: As it was Plaide by the Right Honourable the Earle of Darbie, Earle of Pembroke, and Earle of Sussex their Seruants . . . London, printed by John Danter' (Chambers: I: 312). Only one copy of this Quarto is known to exist and is today at the Folger Library. Henslowe's diary records performances on 24 December 1593 and on 28 January, 4 February and 5 and 12 June 1594 by the Lord Admiral's and Lord Chamberlain's Men (Foakes: 21–22).

There is also a Quarto copy of the play (Q2) printed in 1600 which is almost, but not exactly, the same as the earlier Quarto. Two copies of Q2 are known to be extant. More common is the 1611 Third Quarto (Q3) that provides a few corrections to the previous Quartos. *Titus Andronicus*, based on Q3, appears in the *First Folio*. For a long time, owing to the horrific nature of its subject matter, scholars and critics tried to deny that Shakespeare wrote the play. John Bailey (1864–1931), President of the English Association in 1926, wrote in 1929: 'Of *Titus Andronicus* I need say nothing, as scarcely anyone thinks Shakespeare wrote it' (cited Vickers, *Shakespeare, Co-Author*: 156). However, subsequently, 'over the last eighty years scholars have applied . . . twenty-one separate tests to the play, each of which has confirmed the presence of a co-author' (Vickers, *Shakespeare, Co-Author*: 243). These tests range from thought and diction parallels, the extent of feminine endings compared with those in the works of Shakespeare's contemporary dramatists, the use of Latinisms and classical allusions and the parallelism of theme and situation, repetitions 'clichés and tricks' (see Vickers, *Shakespeare, Co-Author*: 168–169), parallel passages and so on. These coincide with passages in the poems and plays of George Peele (1556–1596).

Educated at Christ's Hospital and Christ Church, Oxford, Peele is known for his dramatic work and accomplishments in translations from Greek and Latin and an interest in antiquity. His early poem based on Trojan history, *The Tale of Troy*, appeared in print in 1589. Four of his extant plays survive, including *The Arraignment of Paris* (1584), in which he again drew upon an episode in the Trojan saga. Additionally, Peele devised pageants and spectacles for the Mayor of the city of London and wrote verse for special occasions such as the departure of Francis Drake (1540–1596) and others on a naval mission against Spain. 'In the poems as in the plays, Peele develops a variety of English verse forms, not least a newly powerful and supple blank verse' (Reid Barbour: *ODNB*), and his work is included in Elizabethan poetic anthologies.

Today, Peele is remembered for his dramas, including the undated *The Battle of Alcazar* which draws upon patriotic themes. It was acted by the Lord Admiral's Servants and is found in a 1594 edition. Part of the play centres upon a 'renegade English Catholic' named Thomas Stukeley, who intended 'to seize Ireland in rebellion' against Queen Elizabeth. The play uses a presenter as a commentator, a device Shakespeare also used in *Henry V*, 'and the foreshadowing of the dumb show' found most notably in *Hamlet*. 'The themes of the play could not be more familiar to Elizabethan audiences: the perils of illegitimate succession, of rebellion, and of ambition.'

Peele's *Edward I*, published in 1593, contains strong anti-Catholic characterization of *Queen Elinor* and is noted for its use of spectacle, including the attempt to dramatically depict the sinking of a ship. Its title page announces the 'sinking of Queene *Elinor*, who sunck *at Charingcrosse, and rose againe at Pottershith*, now named Queenehith.' The play draws upon blank verse, tetrameter couplets and prose. *The Old Wives Tale*, published in 1595, includes comedy, folk tales, history and allegorical names. *The Love of King David and Fair Bethsabe: With the Tragedy of Absalom* belonging to the 1592–1594 period and published in 1599, draws upon biblical themes and the David, Ammon, Absalom triangle of adultery, treachery, rape, incest and rebellion.

Peele's connections extended from the very powerful statesman and spymaster William Cecil, Lord Burghley (1520/21–1598), the Earl of Oxford (1550–1604), to the London literary world. The critic and clergyman Francis Meres, in his account of his literary contemporaries *Palladis Tamia,* includes Peele among the galaxy of England's finest poets and dramatic tragedians. Peele seems to have died in poverty, un-respected, representing 'for some of his contemporaries the perils of waste in an Elizabethan literary life begun in scholarship, offered out for patronage, and ended in the squalor of a professional playwright's meagre existence' (*ODNB*).

Peele's, rhetoric 'monotonous verse, stilted diction, and constant self-repetition' (Vickers, *Shakespeare, Co-Author*: 206), use of classicism and other stylistic features, reveal him as Shakespeare's co-author of *Titus Andronicus*. Shakespeare's reasons for working with Peele must remain speculative. Perhaps the young apprentice dramatist thought he could learn and benefit from working with the slightly older and more experienced university trained Peele and that from him he could reinforce and verify the use of classical allusion in the tragedy.

Timon of Athens

Shakespeare's collaboration with others is not limited to his early works, but also reflected in the tragedies. *Timon of Athens* is a tragedy of isolation and ingratitude. Timon's so-called friends take from him when he has power and affluence and then reject him after his reversal of fortune. The once-generous Timon is transformed into a misogynist. The play's 'central structure has an icy clarity-and it is all about ingratitude.' There is 'an extraordinary subtle structure' (Nuttall: 313, 315). However, since the early nineteenth century, there has been speculation, due to oddities in the play, that it is not solely by Shakespeare. Part of its authorship has been identified with Thomas Middleton. Common to Middleton's work and rare in Shakespeare are the number of characters in *Timon of Athens*, such as the Poet, the Painter, the Fool, the Merchant and others, who have a prominent part in the play but lack personal names. Also, irregularities of the verse, use of rhyming couplets and unmetrical blank verse are more characteristic of Middleton than Shakespeare. The scholarly consensus today is that Shakespeare focused on the start of the play, the scenes with Timon himself and the ending.

On the other hand, Middleton wrote at least the second scene of the opening act and the third act. Such an attribution is based upon Middleton's use of language, oaths, the spelling in the early printed text, vocabulary and peculiarities of prose and verse. No external evidence appeared on the play prior to its appearance in the 1623 *First Folio*. The text itself is replete with irregularities, loose plot ends, lineation issues and curious pronoun usage. There is also a gap in the page numbering in the Folio between *Timon of Athens* and the play that follows it, *Julius Caesar*. Scholars have argued that this space was reserved for *Troilus and Cressida*, which has led to speculation that *Timon of Athens* was going to be omitted but was included in the Folio at the last moment (see Hinman, II: 280–285). Be that as it may, 'authorship studies from the 1840s to the 1990s,' utilizing very different methods combined with the 'newest statistical methods', according to Vickers, 'agree in assigning to Middleton a substantial part of *Timon* and Shakespeareans who continue to deny this point risk forfeiting their scholarly credibility' (*Shakespeare, Co-Author*: 290).

The question remains why Shakespeare collaborated with the younger Thomas Middleton. In *Shakespeare and Co.* (2006), Stanley Wells's study of Shakespeare and his contemporary dramatists, Wells speculates that Shakespeare may have been ill during the 1605–1606 period during which Wells believes *Timon of Athens* to be written. Possibly, Shakespeare 'may simply have wished to encourage a younger colleague' or the 'play's success when performed by the King's Men – quite possibly with Shakespeare in the cast – encouraged him to accept Middleton, sixteen years his junior, as a kind of senior apprentice' (154).

Thomas Middleton

The publication of Thomas Middleton's *The Collected Works* and *Thomas Middleton and Early Modern Textual Culture: A Companion to The Collected Works* (2007) provides the foundation for the reassessment of Middleton's life, individual and collaborative work, and achievement. In spite of the praise of, for instance, A. C. Swinburne (1837–1909), T. S. Eliot (1885–1965) and others, Middleton suffered from centuries of neglect. His plays were rarely performed and the King's Men did not turn to him as their leading dramatist when, in the late years of the first decade of the seventeenth century, Shakespeare seems to have begun to withdraw from the theatrical world and devoted more of his time to Stratford-upon-Avon.

Timon of Athens seems to have been Shakespeare's only substantial collaboration with Middleton, although portions of *Macbeth* have also been attributed to Middleton. According to Middleton's modern advocate, Gary Taylor, Middleton's dramas were regarded as too bawdy. Middleton 'is the only other Renaissance playwright', apart from Shakespeare, 'who created acknowledged masterpieces of comedy, tragedy, and history; his revolutionary English history play, *A Game of Chess*, was also the greatest box-office hit of early modern London.' Taylor writes, 'Middleton's sexed language, and languaged sex, more comprehensively than creatively than any other writer in English.' According to Taylor, Middleton dramatized incest, the allure of the male transvestite, stalking and sexual blackmail, castration, sexually abusive priests, marital rape, male impotence, masochism, necrophilia and paedophilia. Further, his reputation probably was affected by the fact that his plays were not collected in his lifetime or immediately after his death in 1627, whereas the existence of collected Folio works gave Ben Jonson, Shakespeare and Beaumont and Fletcher an advantage. The first collected Middleton did not appear until 1840 (Taylor and Lavagnino, *The Collected Works*: [2], 25, 58).

It is claimed that there are four reasons for Middleton's greatness. Shakespeare and he are the only playwrights of their period to write great comedies, tragedies, histories and tragicomedies. Secondly, Middleton's plays are replete with insights into the everyday life led by late sixteenth and early seventeenth-century Londoners. Thirdly, Middleton's treatment of sexuality is more comprehensive than any other 'writer in English'. Fourthly, his work contains 'a daring proto-modernity and intense individualization of character' (J. Bate, *TLS*, April 25, 2008, 3: reviewing Taylor and Lavagnino).

According to Gary Taylor, 'no English writer before Middleton had ever achieved such complex sustained transparency, such seemingly unconstructed representation of the shifting currents of speech' (*ODNB*). Who was this genius? Born into a prosperous London background, he is named early on in a lawsuit and his works are full of satire on the legal profession. In 1598, he was at Queen's College,

Oxford, but soon drifted into the London literary world. His first work was dedicated to the Earl of Essex and published in 1597. Writing profusely in various genres, including pamphlets, poems and plays, he was sufficiently well-established by 1602 to collaborate with Thomas Dekker, and he fell foul of the influential Ben Jonson, who became a lifelong enemy.

In 1603, he made a well-connected marriage to the daughter of a clerk in the Court of Chancery. He survived the plague and wrote plays that were published rather than performed and continued to collaborate with Dekker on a popular drama such as *The Black Book*. This was published in 1604 and stayed in print and on the stage for 30 years. Other works followed, including *A Trick to Catch the Old One* (1605) and the superb *The Revenger's Tragedy* (sometimes ascribed to Cyril Tourneur). He continued to produce well into the 1620s and had a close association with the King's Men. His most successful play, *A Game of Chess*, was performed at the Globe between the 5–14 August 1624. Thereafter, his work and life seemed to have deteriorated. Deeply in debt, he was buried on 4 July 1627, 'his impoverished widow survived him by only a year' (*ODNB*). His career exemplifies the diversity and vitality of the late Elizabeth-Jacobean theatrical scene and insecurities of the life of the writer.

Pericles, Prince of Tyre

A further drama displaying evidence of Shakespeare working with another dramatist is *Pericles, Prince of Tyre*. It was entered in the Stationers' Register on 20 May 1608 by Edward Blount (1564–1632), the bookseller and publisher who participated in the production of the *First Folio*. Blount described it as 'a booke called the booke of Pericles prynce of Tyre', however no Quarto was printed by Blount. Perhaps he entered the title in order to attempt to stop anyone else from publishing it. Also in 1608, George Wilkins (d. 1618), the dramatist and pamphleteer, published a prose romance, *The Painful Adventures of Pericles, Prince of Tyre*. This is described as 'the true History of the Play of Pericles, as it was lately presented by the worthy and ancient Poet John Gower.' This was performed 'by the King's Majesty's Players', in other words, Shakespeare's company. The Venetian and French ambassadors to London accompanied one another to a performance between May 1606 and November 1608 (*Riverside*: 1527).

The play was very popular, in fact something of a theatrical hit. Apparently in 1609, there was a large audience for a performance. In 1619, there was an elaborate quasi-government sponsored production with a banquet during an extended interval at which visiting dignitaries were lavishly entertained. Ben Jonson, not without a note of jealousy, in his 'Ode to Himself' (1629) described *Pericles, Prince of Tyre* as a 'mouldy tale', and two years later, he complains that the play was selling more than his own work.

Inevitably, pirated published texts appeared. Henry Gosson (d. 1640), the London publisher and bookseller, published probably his sole play text capitalizing on the popularity of *Pericles, Prince of Tyre*. His non-authorized Quarto (Q1) appeared in 1609, as did a second edition (Q2) of the play, making it with *Richard II* one of the two Shakespeare's plays to be published in a Quarto version in the same year. In fact, Q1 was reprinted three times before the publication of the 1623 *First Folio* and there were also Quartos published in 1630 and 1635. However, the play doesn't appear in the *First Folio*. The reasons for this are unclear as it is printed in the Third Folio published in 1664. The Norton Edition editor observes that 'Because all editions ultimately derive from Q1, *Pericles* occupies a unique status.' The editor adds that, 'For every other Shakespearean play with the ambiguous exception of *Richard III*, at least one early printed early version apparently draws directly on an authorial manuscript or a scribal transcript of it, such as a promptbook.' However, 'since no reasonably authoritative text of *Pericles* exists, even the claim that Q1 is a report of a performance cannot depend on comparison with a presumably more accurate version but must rely on internal evidence alone' (2731).

Exceedingly popular theatrically in the early seventeenth century, it was the first of Shakespeare's plays to receive a revival when the London theatres were reopened after the Civil War. It proved not to be popular and was ignored until a 1738 adaptation. The fairy-tale elements and pageantry attracted some late twentieth-century productions, and there is at the time of this writing only one full-length film or TV version: the BBC-TV production of 1983. It should not be forgotten that the recognition scene in which the King recognizes his long lost daughter inspired T. S. Eliot so much that one of his most moving poems, 'Marina' (1930), is based upon it.

The critical history of the play since the late seventeenth century has emphasized its formal flaws rather than its powerful depiction of reconciliation and recognition after all has seemed lost. For Dryden, in his *An Essay on the Dramatic Poetry of the Last Age* (1672), the plot contained 'lameness', the story was 'ridiculous' and 'incoherent' (cited Dobson and Wells: 344). Nicholas Rowe included *Pericles, Prince of Tyre* in his 1709 edition of Shakespeare's plays and poems. Rowe's observation has generally been accepted that 'there is good Reason to believe that the greatest part of that Play was not written by him [Shakespeare]; tho' it is own'd that some part of it certainly was, particularly the last Act' (cited Vickers, *Shakespeare, Co-Author*: [291]). In a detailed, judicious assessment of the evidence, Vickers concludes that 'the whole weight of scholarship [exists] proving that Shakespeare was one of the play's two co-authors' (327).

George Wilkins

The *Pericles* co-author was George Wilkins, who largely wrote the first two acts and closely collaborated with Shakespeare on the rest of the play and especially the brothel scenes.[11] Little is known about Wilkins' life. His father was a poet. The son's first known published work, *The History of Justine* (1606), drew heavily upon Arthur Golding's (?1536–?1605) earlier translation of the Roman chronicle. Wilkins' *The Miseries of Enforced Marriage* was performed in 1607 by the King's Men. The Queen's Men in the same year performed Wilkins', John Day's (c.1574–c.1640) and William Rowley's (c.1585–1626) *The Travels of the Three English Brothers*. In other words, Wilkins was known as a dramatic collaborator. He also was associated with Recusancy and Catholic families (see Anthony Parr's entry on Wilkins in the *ODNB*).

Henry Gosson, the publisher of *Pericles, Prince of Tyre*, also published Wilkins' *Three Miseries of Barbary* (?1607), and Gosson stood bail for Wilkins in 1611 when the latter was accused of assault. Wilkins' *The Painful Adventures of Pericles, Prince of Tyre* (1608) drew heavily upon the play of *Pericles, Prince of Tyre*. After the publication of the play, there is no other evidence of Wilkins' subsequent connection with the King's Men. In fact, from 1610 onwards, he was frequently cited in court cases and ran an inn, probably also a brothel, in a distinctly red light area of London. Gosson put up bail for Wilkins who was accused of 'abusing one Randall Borkes and kicking a woman on the belly which was then great with child.'

Known as violent, he and Shakespeare in 1612 were both called as witnesses in the Mountjoy-Bellot case. In a 1614 case in which his wife was involved, a witness gave testimony that 'Wilkins' house was frequented by lewd women.' Two years later, he gave court testimony against rioters who pulled down some of his house: 'almost certainly an example of the action habitually directed against theatres and brothels'. In 1618, accused of protecting a felon, he was discharged on 2 October as 'he is dead' (cited in Parr). Wilkins' life in some ways resembles the play he collaborated on, *Pericles, Prince of Tyre*. Pericles' life is one of extremes, of imprisonment, brothels, release from imprisonment, achievement and failure. For Wilkins, however, in life there was no burial alive at sea or miraculous, magical restoration that occurs in the drama. No supernatural forces entered in his life as they do in *Pericles* to rescue the central protagonists from despair and disaster.

Cardenio, Henry VIII (All Is True) *and* The Two Noble Kinsmen

Cardenio

Further evidence of Shakespeare working in collaboration is provided by three late plays, although the text of one, in common with the probably earlier *Love's Labour's Won,* hasn't survived. On 20 May 1613, the Privy Council approved the sum of £20 to be paid to John Heminges (1566–1630), the head of the King's Men. The payment was for court performances of six plays, one of these being 'Cardenno.' On 9 July 1613, Heminges was paid £6. 13s 4d for the King's Men's performance of a drama 'called Cardenna' acted in the presence of the ambassador of the Dukedom of Savoy. Over 40 years later, on 9 September 1653, a London publisher Humphrey Moseley (d. 1661)

entered into the Stationers' Register (he was a freeman of the Stationers' company) some plays. These included '*The History of Cardenio*,
by Mr. Fletcher and Shakespeare'. Cardenio was a character found
in the first part of Cervantes' (1547–1616) *Don Quixote* (1605)
that appeared in an English translation in 1612. Interestingly, Lewis
Theobald (1688–1744), an important Shakespearean scholar and
editor, in 1728 published a play entitled *Double Falsehood, or The
Distrest Lovers*. He claimed he had 'revised and adapted' it from a
play 'originally written by W. Shakespeare'. The play has a 'disguised
heroine wronged by her lover, the hero's descent into madness, and
the ultimate restoration of sundered relationships', reminiscent of
Shakespeare's late plays (*Norton*: 3117).

All is True (Henry VIII)

All is True or *Henry VIII* seems ill-fated. On 29 June 1613 during
a Globe performance, a canon fired to herald the King's appearance
in the fourth scene of the first act, caused a fire that destroyed the
theatre. This was probably the fourth performance of the play. There
are five known accounts of the fire. Three refer to the play as 'All is
True' and the other two 'the play of Henry 8'. In the 1623 *First Folio*
it appears as the last of the 'Histories' under the title *The Famous
History of the Life of King Henry the Eighth*, and with the probable
exception of the slightly later *The Two Noble Kinsmen* (1613–1614),
is regarded as Shakespeare's last play. Both are collaboratively written
with John Fletcher.

The Fletcher collaboration on *Henry VIII* has largely been accepted
since the middle of the nineteenth century. The attribution is based
on stylistic and linguistic foundations, including analysis of vocabulary, verse, colloquial forms, and grammatical constructions. The
general consensus is that Fletcher wrote the Prologue, the third
and fourth scenes of the first act, the first scene of act three and
scenes two, three and four of the final act. He may, too, have revised
Shakespeare's first two scenes of the second act, parts of the second
scene of the third act, and the first two scenes of the fourth act.

Charles Lamb (1775–1834), writing in his *Specimens of English
Dramatic Poets* (1808), succinctly identifies the stylistic differences

between Fletcher and Shakespeare. The former 'lays line upon line, making up one after another, adding image to image so deliberately that we see where they join. Shakespeare mingles everything, embarrasses sentences and metaphors'. Lamb adds, 'before one has burst its shell, another is hatched and clamours for this disclosure' (478: cited Vickers, *Shakespeare, Co-Author*: 362).

These distinctions are found in two contrasting representative passages from the play, each dealing with a similar issue: Henry's intention to seek a divorce from Queen Katherine. In the second scene of the second act, Norfolk tells Suffolk and the Lord Chamberlain that Henry

> . . . counsels a divorce, a loss of her
> That, like a jewel, has hung twenty years
> About his neck, yet never lost her lustre;
> Of her that loves him with that excellence [great virtue]
> That angels love good men with; even of her
> That when the greatest stroke [severest blow] of fortune falls,
> Will bless the King. (30–36)

According to R. A. Law in his 'The Double Authorship of *Henry VIII*', *Studies in Philology*, 56 (1959), in this passage attributed to Fletcher, 'here we have in simple direct language the thought expressed with three images separately developed.' By way of contrast is the scene that follows. In the opening eleven lines attributed to Shakespeare, 'exactly the same thought is put into the mouth of unsophisticated Anne Boleyn.' In these lines (2. 3. 1–11), 'at least five images are mingled in complex sentences by the maid of honor sympathizing with her mistress' (478–479: cited Vickers, *Shakespeare, Co-Author*: 363).

The play contains lengthy, detailed stage directions, many episodes breaking up the continuity of the action, various rhetorical speeches rather than extensive character depiction and is concerned with, as its refrain and alternative title *All is True* suggests, the apparent historical truth. The play was frequently performed before the Civil War and from 1664 onwards. In the eighteenth and nineteenth centuries, its pageantry and spectacle particularly appealed. However, in the twentieth century, the play fell out of favour. Critics tended to dismiss it as a display piece for pomp and rhetoric. Late twentieth-century perspectives, in addition to the revived scholarly interest in its authorship, have focused on its apparent sympathetic portrait of Queen Katherine and a seemingly sceptical element in its treatment of Tudor politics.[12]

The Two Noble Kinsmen

There is less controversy concerning the co-authorship of Shakespeare's probable final theatrical work. Excluded from the 1623 *First Folio*, probably owing to its being a collaborative work, *The Two Noble Kinsmen* was entered in the Stationers' Register for 8 April 1634: 'a Tragi Comedy called the two noble kinsmen by John Fletcher and William Shakespeare'. A Quarto edition was also published in the same year. Its title page reads: 'The Two Noble Kinsmen: Presented at the Blackfriars by the Kings Majesties servants, with great applause'. It adds, 'written by the memorable worthies of their time: Mr. John Fletcher and Mr. William Shakespeare . . . Printed at London by Tho. Cotes for John Waterson . . . 1634'.

Attempts to distinguish Shakespeare's contribution from Fletcher's have preoccupied scholars and critics. The consensus is that Shakespeare probably wrote the first act, the first scene of the second, the opening two scenes of the third act and a good deal of the final act, Fletcher wrote the rest plus the Prologue and the Epilogue. Shakespeare seems to have focused on the framework narrative relating to Theseus, and the beginning and ending of the plot relating to the cousins Palamon and Arcite. Primarily a dramatization of Chaucer's 'Knight's Tale', *The Two Noble Kinsmen* is a complicated tragicomedy 'of a medieval English tale [Chaucer] based on an Italian romance version of a Latin epic about one of the oldest and most tragic Greek legends.' It explores 'complex issues of same-sex intimacy and social coercion.'[13]

The dating of *The Two Noble Kinsmen* has been assigned to the years 1613–1614. Such dating is based upon Act 3, Scene 5, with its rural entertainment largely taken from Francis Beaumont's *Masque of the Inner Temple and Gray's Inn*, staged on 20 February 1613. The final line of the 'Prologue' of *The Two Noble Kinsmen* refers to 'Our losses fall so thick we must needs leave' (31): in other words, probably to the fire of June 1613 that razed the Globe to the ground. Further, Ben Jonson's *Bartholomew Fair* had its initial performance in October 1614 and makes allusions to Palamon, a central figure in *The Two Noble Kinsmen*.

Francis Beaumont and John Fletcher

What was Shakespeare's connection with John Fletcher, who after 1613 probably took the former's place as the leading dramatist for the King's company? By 1613, Fletcher's long standing collaborative personal and professional partnership with Francis Beaumont disintegrated. Beaumont married in 1613, had two daughters, and retired from theatrical activity. He died on 6 March 1616, two months before Shakespeare. Fletcher, on the other hand, went on writing and collaborating, maintaining his connection with the King's company until the 1620s. A bachelor from a well-connected clerical Protestant background with court connections, he was a close relative of Giles Fletcher (?1549–1611), who served as a diplomat, wrote poetry including sonnet sequences and was caught up in the Essex rebellion. A Cambridge graduate, John Fletcher was close to Ben Jonson, who was, according to a prefatory poem by Richard Brome (*c.*1590–1653) in the 1647 Folio of Fletcher's works, 'proud to call him Sonne' (cited Fletcher *ODNB* entry).

Conclusion

Fletcher and Beaumont probably wrote for the King's company, Shakespeare's group, from 1608 onwards: 'None of Fletcher's plays after 1614 can be shown to have been written for any other company' (Ibid.). Fletcher also drew heavily on Shakespeare's *The Taming of the Shrew* for *The Woman's Prize*, which he wrote single-handedly and dates from around 1612. In short, Fletcher was a very highly skilled and well-respected professional dramatist who collaborated with the older, very experienced senior dramatist of the company, Shakespeare. Both were closely associated with the King's Men. To summarize, the writers with whom Shakespeare worked, included in this review of Shakespeare as collaborator, George Peele, Thomas Middleton, George Wilkins and John Fletcher, were all professionals, and with, the exception of Peele, possessed considerable theatrical experience. Further, the evidence of Shakespeare's handwriting provided by *Sir Thomas More* demonstrates Shakespeare's craftsmanship, skill in writing out dramatic materials and awareness that they probably required further additions. Above all, metrical, verbal and textual evidence shows Shakespeare to have been more inventive, innovative, to possess greater consummate skill than his collaborators. He was the better handler of his source materials. Shakespeare was the greater dramatist.

Chapter Nine
The Last Years: The Late Romances

The Final Years

1611

Around 1610, it is thought that Shakespeare spent a good deal more time in Stratford than in London. In 1611, he and others are preoccupied defending their Stratford tithes and other properties in the Court of Chancery against other claimants. Two of Shakespeare's plays were performed at court in Whitehall: *The Tempest*, acted on 'Hallomas night', 1 November 1611, and *The Winter's Tale* on 5 November 1611. Seeing performances at the Globe of *Macbeth* on 20 April [1611], Simon Forman also recorded witnessing *Cymbeline* at an unnamed time and venue, *Richard II* on 30 April 1611 and *The Winter's Tale* on 15 May 1611 (*Riverside*: 1966–1968).

These plays competed with others in a highly competitive theatrical world. Leading competitors included Thomas Dekker's *Match Me in London* (1611), John Fletcher's *The Night Walker, or the Little Thief* (not published until 1640), Ben Jonson's *Catiline His Conspiracy* (1611), and Thomas Middleton's *No Wit, No Help Like a Woman's* (1611) and *A Chaste Maid in Cheapside* (*c.*1611).

Literary activity in 1611 was not confined to the theatre. The year also witnessed the publication of John Donne's (*c.*1571–1631), (*The First Anniversary) An Anatomy of the World* and the eminent cartographer and historian John Speed's (?1552–1629) *The Theatre of the Empire of Great Britain*, which included 54 maps and a description accompanying the individual maps. Speed's *History of Great Britain* (1611), encompassing the Roman conquest through to James I's reign, was probably a source for the collaborative *All Is True* (*Henry VIII*).

123

1612

The year 1612 is probably the year of *All Is True* (*Henry VIII*) the lost *Cardenio*. It is also the year of John Webster's (1580–1634) magnificent drama *The White Devil* and various Beaumont and Fletcher collaborations. Other creative endeavours included the first part of Michael Drayton's (1563–1631) celebration of the country, *PolyOlbion, or A Chorographical Description of Great Britain*, Orlando Gibbons' (1583–1623) *First Set of Madrigals and Motets*, and John Dowland's (?1563–?1626) *A Pilgrim's Solace*.

1613

Shakespeare's younger brother Richard (1574–1613), about whom very little is known, died and was buried on 4 February 1613. Somewhat surprisingly, given the tradition that Shakespeare was spending more time in Stratford, on 10 March 1613 he purchased Blackfriars Gatehouse from Henry Walker (d. 1616), an eminent London musician, for the comparatively large sum of £140. This was more than Shakespeare had previously paid for New Place, his prestigious Stratford-upon-Avon dwelling.

The purchase of Shakespeare's only known London property, for which he initially paid £80, is curious. Shakespeare's signature is on the mortgage deed dated 11 March 1613. He also signed a deed to the effect that the complete purchase amount would be paid at Michaelmas on 29 September; however, the mortgage remained unpaid when Shakespeare died in 1616. According to Richard Frith, a Blackfriars resident writing in 1586, Blackfriars Gatehouse 'hath sundry back doors and bye-ways, and many secret vaults and corners'. Frith added, 'It hath been in time past suspected and searched for papists but no good done for want of good knowledge of the back doors and bye-ways, and of the dark corners' (Dobson and Wells: 49).

While Shakespeare put up the money for the purchase, others were involved too, including a William Johnson, the probable landlord of the famous Mermaid Tavern, the haunt of aristocrats, intellectuals and writers. Also involved was a John Jackson, who had connections with John Heminges, the distinguished actor and then business manager for the King's Men. Shakespeare mortgaged the property back to Walker, forming a kind of trusteeship. This would have the consequences of preventing Shakespeare's widow from any claim on the property. In Shakespeare's will, the house, in which Shakespeare probably never lived, was let to a John Robinson, about whom little, if anything, is known.

On 31 March 1613, Shakespeare received 44 shillings for supplying an *impresa,* or emblem and motto, for Francis Manners, 6th Earl of Rutland (1578–1632). There is also a record of the same amount in gold paid 'To Richard Burbage for painting and making it', that is, 'the shield carried by the Earl of Rutland in the tilt at Court on the King's Accession day, 24 March' (Schoenbaum: 18–19). Such evidence reveals that Shakespeare's name commanded very high fees and that he still worked in close collaboration with Burbage, the leading Shakespearean actor of the time.

As noted, on 29 June 1613, the Globe Theatre burnt down. In the theatrical world, 1613 also witnessed Francis Beaumont's *Masque of the Inner Temple and Gray's Inn,* the more than likely source for parts of *The Two Noble Kinsmen* and John Fletcher and Beaumont's *The Scornful Lady.* Non-dramatic work included Thomas Campion's (1567–1620) *Songs of Mourning Bewailing the Death of Prince Henry.* The eldest son of King James and Anne of Denmark, Henry Frederick, Prince of Wales, from whom much was expected, had died from typhoid fever the previous year.

This was also a year of political intrigue and scandal at the Court of King James. Henry's sister Elizabeth (1596–1662) married Frederick, the Elector Palatine (1596–1632), and subsequently King of Bohemia. The pre-wedding celebrations included the performance of twenty plays in a period of three months. Eight of these were by Shakespeare. In the world of court intrigue, the ascendancy of Robert Carr (c.1587–1645), a Scot and favourite of the King, continued: he became Earl of Somerset and married the youthful Countess of Essex (1590–1632). Her divorce, more or less forced upon her by the King, from the young Earl of Essex (1591–1646), created a scandal. This was acerbated by the poisoning of Sir Thomas Overbury (1581–1613) in the Tower of London. Overbury had opposed the marriage. The exposure of the murderers in 1615 and 1616 by Edward Coke (1552–1634) and Francis Bacon led eventually to the downfall of Carr and his wife Lady Essex. Overbury's satirical poem *The Wife* was published in 1614; there were six editions in a year.

1614–1615

John Cobbe (b. before 1561–1614), a wealthy Stratfordian died in 1614, and left Shakespeare the by no means inconsiderable sum for the time of £5. However, in the final two years of his life, Shakespeare became embroiled in arguments relating to the enclosing of land whose tithes he owned in the Stratford area, and especially in Welcombe, a small village roughly a mile and a half from Stratford.

In 1614, the Globe Theatre reopened and Philip Henslowe and his partner Jacob Meade, the waterman and landowner, opened the Hope Theatre on Bankside. John Webster's great play *The Duchess of Malfi* was probably written this year. Sir Walter Raleigh's *The History of the World* was published. King James summoned the parliament known as 'The Addled' for its refusal to do his bidding; James dissolved it. Increasingly out of favour at court, Carr was being replaced as the King's favourite by George Villiers (1592–1628), subsequently the Duke of Buckingham. In 1615, the Overbury scandal occupied the domestic court news and Raleigh yet again fell into disfavour with the king. Middleton's *More Dissemblers Besides Women* was probably written during this time.

1616 and Shakespeare's Death

The year saw the fall of Coke for his persistent opposition to James I, and William Harvey (1578–1657) first expounded his idea concerning the circulation of blood. Francis Beaumont and Philip Henslowe died. On 10 February, Shakespeare's daughter Judith married Thomas Quiney. Their first son, 'Shaksper', was christened on 23 November, died and was buried on 8 May 1617. On 25 March 1616, Shakespeare made his will. He was buried on 25 April in the Stratford-upon-Avon churchyard. Legend has it that he died on 23 April, the same day and month as his birth in 1564. John Ward (1629–1681), Vicar of Stratford from 1662 to 1681, noted that Stratford legend claimed that 'Shakespeare, Drayton, and Ben Jonson had a merry meeting, and it seems, drank too hard, for Shakespeare died of a feavour there contracted' (Dobson and Wells: 516). The epitaph on Shakespeare's tomb warned others to leave his bones where they lay and not to remove them.

> Good frend for Jesu sake forbeare,
> To dig the Dust that lyeth incloased here
> Blessed is the man, that spareth these stones
> Cursed be he yt moveth these bones (Chambers: II: 250).

This probably is Shakespeare's warning to the Stratford sexton not to dig up his bones and dump them in the charnel house next to the church.

Shakespeare's Will

Shakespeare's will has been the subject of much speculation. It was probably drafted by Shakespeare's lawyer, Francis Collins (d. 1617), who received a legacy from Shakespeare of £13. 6s. 8d. in January 1616, before the February 1616 marriage of Shakespeare's daughter Judith to Thomas Quiney. A month later, a Margaret Wheeler died having given birth to Quiney's child. Quiney admitted in the ecclesiastical court to fornication. Instead of public penance, he paid a fine of 5 shillings. In March 1616, Shakespeare's will was changed and the alterations largely relate to Judith.

The will is dated 25 March 1616 and is today in the Public Record Office at Kew. The main bequests are:

1. To his daughter Judith, £100 as a marriage portion. Another £50 would be hers provided she relinquished her rights to Susannah, her sister, in a cottage in Chapel Lane, Stratford. She was also to receive the interest on another £150, or if she died within three years (she lived on until 1662 and had three sons) to her children. The interest was to be hers whilst she was married and her husband could claim only the £150 if he settled land of equivalent value on her. She was also left her father's silver-and-gilt bowl.

2. Joan Hart (d. 1646), Shakespeare's surviving sister, was left £20, her brother's clothes, and the Henley Street House in Stratford while she lived at a minimal annual rent. Her three sons were left £5 each. Her husband, William Hart, died a week before Shakespeare died.

3. Elizabeth Hall (1608–1670), Shakespeare's grand-daughter, eight at the time of his death, was left most of his silver. Following her mother Susannah's death in 1649, she inherited more of her grandfather's estate and lived in New Place. Her first husband, Thomas Nash (1593–1647), the elder son of Shakespeare's friend Anthony Nash (d. 1622), is buried next to Shakespeare in the Holy Trinity Church Stratford chancel.

4. Shakespeare left the relatively small sum of £10 for the Stratford Poor.

5. Thomas Combe (1589–1657), a member of an influential Protestant Stratford family, and a bachelor, was left Shakespeare's sword. There were also other related small bequests to local friends.

6. Hamnet Sadler (d. 1624), a friend of Shakespeare's and a witness to the will, received 26s. 8d. to purchase a mourning ring. Shakespeare's godson, William Walker (1608–1680), received 20 shillings in gold.

7. Shakespeare left 26s. 8d. to three of his 'fellows' in the King's Men: Richard Burbage, John Heminges and Henry Condell (bap. 1576–1627), the actor and subsequently editor of the *First Folio*.

8. Susannah (Hall), Shakespeare's daughter, received almost everything else, although provision was made for any sons she might have. In fact, Elizabeth was her only child, and then the property went to Judith and her future sons.

9. Susannah and her husband, John, were appointed executors. They received the household goods. These included Shakespeare's books and papers, which are not mentioned in the will.

Interlineated as an afterthought on the third and last sheet of the will is the following: 'Item I gyve unto my wief my second-best bed with the furniture.' The second-best bed might have been the marriage bed, with the best bed in the house being the one where guests slept. It is unclear whether Anne would have received one-third of her late husband's estate, as was the custom in London, York and Wales. The will's lack of explicitness on the matter has given grounds to much speculation. Burbage's will refers to his 'well beloved' wife and she acted as the executor. Henry Condell left all his property to his 'well beloved' wife.[14]

Germaine Greer in *Shakespeare's Wife* gives a judicious account of various explanations put forward concerning the will. She quotes Edmond Malone's observation that Shakespeare's 'wife had not wholly escaped his memory, he had forgot her, he had recollected her, as more strongly to mark how little he esteemed her; he had already . . . cut her off, not indeed with a shilling but with an old bed' (322). As Peter Holland in his *ODNB* entry on Shakespeare judiciously observes, 'The lack in Shakespeare's will of even a conventional term of endearment, of specific and substantial bequests to Anne, or even of the right to continue living in New Place amounts to a striking silence.'

The Romances: Cymbeline, The Winter's Tale, The Tempest

Pericles, Cymbeline, The Winter's Tale and *The Tempest*, along with the co-authored *The Two Noble Kinsmen*, were published for the first time in the *First Folio*. They don't conclude with the deaths of all the main protagonists and combine tragic elements with the comedies' seemingly unifying resolutions. They contain romance elements and are known as Shakespeare's late romances. Common to them are elements of separation and the subsequent coming together or reunion of members of the same family.

In *Pericles, Cymbeline, The Winter's Tale* and *The Two Noble Kinsmen*, daughters lose their parents. In the first three, wives are apart from husbands – in *The Tempest* permanently and in *The Winter's Tale*, a son is lost forever. Exile is a common feature. Those who are banished – usually rulers – are restored to their rightful home at the end of the play, with the opportunity to occupy their former positions. Jealousy, too, plays a role. So, too, is the necessity for patience in situations of difficulty. Forgiveness operates, especially in *The Winter's Tale* and *The Tempest*. The plots are episodic and the locations exotic. There are shipwrecks, magic and spectacular theatrical effects. For instance, at the opening of *The Tempest*, a ship breaks up in a tempest (man made, as it emerges).

The romance tradition has its roots in Greek Hellenistic literature in which love initiates often heroic ventures and is put to enormous tests. These may consist of intrigues, jealousy and personal conflicts. A lover may go on a lengthy journey to far away places and encounter mythological creatures, gods and monsters. The protagonists are either noble or royal. In other words, their appeal lay in an escape from the every day into a world of fantasy. One representation of this, at the time of James I, was the elaborate court masque combining music, song, dance, elaborate costumes and stage spectacle, witnessed, for instance, in *The Tempest*. Such theatricals were for indoor, private venues, rather than, for example, the Globe, which was not totally protected from the vagaries of the weather.

The far-away islands and settings of Shakespeare's late plays, with their use of masque elements, make them part of the romance tradition. Shakespeare's lens in these plays is not only on young lovers but on an older generation and on reconciliation rather than revenge. Lovers are introduced by their parents. In order to right a wrong from a previous generation, Prospero introduces his daughter, Miranda, to Ferdinand, the son of his enemy Alonso, wrongful King of Naples who usurped his throne. In the late romances, apparent death and resurrection take place. For instance, in *Cymbeline*, Imogen and Posthumus believe mistakenly, as do Ferdinand and Alonso in *The Tempest*, that the other is dead. In *The Winter's Tale*, Perdita and Hermione are believed dead and Paulina constructs a very elaborate resurrection spectacle.

There are also tragic elements associated more with winter rather than spring in the tragic rather than the comic cycle. There is separation, mourning, errors, conflict, regret and considerable suffering. Pericles, Leontes in *The Winter's Tale*, Cymbeline and Prospero all suffer and are intensely lonely; each has a grievance. Only Prospero is able to retain his daughter. Apart from the co-authored *Pericles*, each drama experiences a final reconciliation that has its consequences for all the participants. There are huge time gaps. In *The Winter's Tale*, 16 years elapse between its first and subsequent action. Similarly, in *The Tempest*, Prospero and his daughter live for more than a decade on the island before Prospero is reconciled with those who drove him away. The struggles giving way to resurrection and reconciliation are represented by a coming together of the new generation, the daughters and sons of enemies.

These romances have their pagan components, too. In *Pericles*, the Goddess Diana appears; in *Cymbeline*, Jupiter; in *The Winter's Tale*, Apollo's oracle is invoked. In the first scene of the fourth act of *The Tempest*, the spirits Iris, Ceres and Juno go through their paces, and in the co-authored *The Two Noble Kinsmen*, in Act 5, Scene 1, there is worship at the altars of the pagan Mars, Venus and Diana. Critics such as G. Wilson Knight in his *The Crown of Life: Essays in Interpretation of Shakespeare's Final Plays* (1947) argue that these late plays constitute allegories of resurrection in Christian terms. The characters are hostages to what Prospero, who acts on the island where he is exiled as a god, describes as 'bountiful Fortune' (1. 2. 178). The play is dominated by shipwrecks and the elemental forces of the ocean. In their adversity, the central figures have to retain the faith that all will be well, or in Paulina's words in *The Winter's Tale*: 'It is requir'd | You do awake your faith' (5. 3. 94–95).

In *The Tempest*, Prospero initiates the action through conjuring up a tempest at sea that brings his enemies to his island exile so that he can forgive them. Imogen in *Cymbeline* is reconciled to Posthumus in spite of his actions; Cymbeline is merciful to his prisoners. Hermione forgives Leontes in *The Winter's Tale*. This spirit of reconciliation and forgiveness has been perceived to be Shakespeare's at the conclusion of his career. For A. D. Nuttall in *Shakespeare the Thinker*, 'although Prospero is not Shakespeare, the possibility of identification is stronger than with other characters.' Nuttall adds, 'Nineteenth-century readers inferred at once that when Prospero promised to drown his book and give up magic, this, occurring as it does in the last of Shakespeare's plays, is the dramatist's farewell to play-making.' For Nuttall, such a notion is not 'sentimental nonsense' (376).

Nuttall does not see *The Tempest* through Christian lenses. Citing Act 1, Scene 2 'Full fadom five thy father lies . . . But doth suffer a sea-change | Into something rich and strange' (397–402), Nuttall reads the play as presenting, 'a picture of eternity that has nothing whatsoever to do with resurrection, Christianity, or life.' Such lines do not associate with 'the enhanced consciousness central to the Christian afterlife,' but rather relate to an 'elimination of consciousness.

Coral and pearl are beautiful, but their beauty is not like that of living men and women; it is the beauty of filigree, jewellery, sculpture, art. Paradise becomes heartless . . . eternal life eternal death' (375–376).

Attention to such matters should not divert attention from the distinct stylistic features of the late romances, so very different from those found in Shakespeare's earlier dramatic writing. In her essay on *The Winter's Tale* in her *Essays, Mainly Shakespearian* (1994), Anne Barton writes that, 'Shakespeare has adjusted his language and dramatic art to the demands of a new mode: one in which plot, on the whole, has become more vivid and emotionally charged than character' (180–181).

Linguistic features that are prominent in the late plays include:

1. Ellipsis or radical compression. Russ McDonald observes in his *Shakespeare's Later Style*: 'Complex ideas are packed into few words, often at the expense of the dominant metrical pattern and the expected syntactical forms' (77). For instance, Ariel informs his master, Prospero, 'Not a hair perish'd; | On their sustaining garments not a blemish, | But fresher than before' (1. 2. 218–219). The first clause omits 'a verbal phrase (*there is*), as does the second (*the garments are*).' The initial 'conditional clauses that Ferdinand blurts out to Miranda' are omitted in his "O, if a virgin, | And your affection not gone forth, I'll make you | The Queen of Naples'" (1. 2. 448–450: McDonald, *Shakespeare's Later Style*: 91).

2. Convoluted syntax with a high frequency of 'deformed phrases, directional shifts, and intricately constructed sentences' (McDonald, *Shakespeare's Later Style*: 33). For instance, Posthumus' lengthy misogynist soliloquy at the opening of the fifth scene of the second act of *Cymbeline* is convoluted to the point of incoherence (1–35).

3. A good deal of parenthesis or many brackets. For instance, in the second scene of *The Tempest*, Prospero reminds Ariel of past history:

> Then was this island
> (Save for the son that [she] did litter here,
> A freckled whelp, hag-born) not honor'd with
> A human shape. (281–284)

4. Repetition, the repetition of 'letters, words, phrases, rhythms'. These become at times 'almost obsessive . . . resounding most audibly in the extraordinary echoing effects of *The Tempest*' (McDonald, *Shakespeare's Later Style*: 33). In his remarkable speech in the second scene of the third act of *The Tempest*, Caliban tells Stephano and Trinculo:

> Be not afeared, the isle is full of noises,
> Sounds, and sweet airs, that give delight and hurt not.
> Sometimes a thousand twangling instruments
> Will hum about mine ears; and sometimes voices,
> That if I then had wak'd after long sleep,
> Will make me sleep again, and then in dreaming,
> The clouds methought would open, and show riches
> Ready to drop upon me, that when I wak'd
> I cried to dream again.

The repetitive sounds, assonance and alliteration, echo and reverberate. See, for instance, the cumulative 'o' and 'd' sounds of the last two lines (135–143).

5. 'Blank verse, usually a guarantor of order and regularity, is now aggressively irregular, encompassing enjambments', that is, run-on lines, 'light or weak endings, frequent stops or shifts of direction, and other threats to the integrity of the line' (McDonald, *Shakespeare's Later Style*: 33). For example, in, Act 2 Scene 1 of *The Winter's Tale,* Hermione observes:

> I am not prone to weeping, as our sex
> Commonly are, the want of which vain dew
> Perchance shall dry your pities; but I have
> That honourable grief lodg'd here which burns
> Worse than tears drown. (108–112)

6. 'Metaphors tend to be introduced and often succeeded rapidly by others, not articulated at length' (McDonald, *Shakespeare's Later Style*: 33). To return to the example from the second scene of *The Tempest*, Prospero reminds Ariel:

    she [Sycorax] did confine thee,
By help of her more potent ministers,
And in her most unmitigable rage,
Into a cloven pine, within which rift
Imprison'd, thou didst painfully remain
A dozen years; within which space she died,
And left thee there, where thou didst vent thy groans
As fast as mill-wheels strike. Then was this island . . .
(274–284)

The metaphors move from 'rift' to 'imprison'd,' then to 'pain', to time, to 'a dozen years', to 'space', death, desertion, to groaning, and to the mechanism of agricultural machinery, and then returns to the island. Prospero's thoughts then transform to those of deformity. Russ McDonald observes: 'governing all these technical features is a pervasive self-consciousness, an artist's playful delight in calling attention to his own virtuosity' (33).

Cymbeline

Simon Forman records that he saw *Cymbeline* performed in April 1611. It first appeared in print in the *First Folio*. Its metre, style, use of romance elements, affinities with Beaumont and Fletcher's play *Philaster* (1609), and non-use of Plutarch upon whom Shakespeare so heavily depended for *Timon of Athens*, *Antony and Cleopatra* and *Coriolanus*, all point to a composition date between 1608 and 1610. Such dating accords with the closing of the London theatres from the summer of 1608 to the end of 1609 due to the plague. No contemporary performance other than Forman's is recorded.

    The Restoration dramatist Thomas D'Urfey (?1653–1723) adapted it as *The Injured Princess, or The Fatal Wager* (1682). This version was revived from time to time until well into the following century. There were elaborate Victorian stagings of *Cymbeline*. Ellen Terry (1847–1928) played a notable Imogen in Henry Irving's (1838–1905), 1896 production. During the twentieth century, it was performed irregularly. A film directed by Elijah Moshinsky (b. 1946), was made in 1982 with Richard Johnson (b. 1927) as the King, Claire Bloom (b. 1931) as the Queen and Helen Mirren (b. 1945) as Imogen.

Cymbeline's concern with Britain's unification in peace within the island and overseas, and its use of masque and setting at Milford Haven on the Welsh coast where Henry VII disembarked to claim the throne, have all been associated with James I, his court and his political agenda. Imogen, in the words of the mid-Victorian commentator Thomas Kenny in 1864, has been perceived as 'undoubtedly the most exquisite of all Shakespeare's female creations' (Dobson and Wells: 103).

Contemporary critical interest traces affinities between *Cymbeline*, its language, motifs, themes, reconciliation elements, reunions and so on, with other plays of Shakespeare's late period.[15] This is, in spite of Dr. Johnson's observation that *Cymbeline* 'has many just sentiments, some natural dialogues, and some pleasing scenes, but they are obtained at the expense of much incongruity'. For Dr. Johnson, 'the folly of the fiction, the absurdity of the conduct, the confusion of the names, and manners of different times', and, he continues at his most strident, 'the impossibility of the events in any system of life, were to waste criticism upon unresisting imbecility, upon faults too evident for detection, and too gross for aggravation' (cited in *Norton*: 2963). George Bernard Shaw (1856–1950) also found *Cymbeline* wanting. His *Cymbeline Refinished* (1936), rewrote the final act retaining '89 lines of Shakespeare's, but none of them spoken by Imogen' (Dobson and Wells: 429).

The Winter's Tale

Simon Forman saw *The Winter's Tale* at the Globe on 15 May 1611. In November 1611, the account books of the Revels' Office record a performance at court by the King's Players of 'Ye Winters night Tayle' (*Riverside*: 1612). In the play, the old shepherd observes that three of the performers had 'danc'd before the King' (4. 4. 337–338). This may well allude to a performance at court of Ben Jonson's *Masque of Oberon,* first played at King James' Court in January 1611 and which also features a dance of three satyrs. Shakespeare drew upon Giovanni

Boccaccio (1313–1375) for both *Cymbeline* and *The Winter's Tale* and especially for the rogue Autolycus' gory telling of the torments apparently lying in wait for the clown (4. 4. 783–791).

The text appears first in the 1623 *First Folio*, where it is placed in the list of the comedies. The play is a retelling of part of Robert Greene's prose romance *Pandosto: The Triumph of Time,* first published in 1588 and which by 1607 had gone into five editions. At the conclusion of Greene's work, Hermione's counterpart (Bellaria) dies and Pandosto (Leontes) kills himself. In other words, Greene's work singularly lacks the element of reconciliation so noteworthy in Shakespeare's adaptation.

In addition to the 1611 Globe performance, *The Winter's Tale* was performed on at least seven occasions at the courts of King James I and his son, Charles I. It was one of the plays performed by the King's Men in 1613 for the wedding festivities of James I's daughter, Princess Elizabeth Stuart. After 1640, the play apparently fell into disfavour and there is no recorded performance until 1741. David Garrick's 1756 production was very popular. There were lavish, spectacular nineteenth-century productions, Charles Kean's (?1811–1868) 1856 production being especially noteworthy. His sets and costumes attempted to duplicate those of ancient Sicily and Bohemia. There were some notable twentieth-century productions, including four film versions, three of these being pre-1915 and silent ones, three television ones and a 1908 operatic version by Karl Goldmark (1830–1915).

The interpretative afterlife of *The Winter's Tale* is not without interest. John Dryden in 1672 dismissed the play in comments also applied to *Measure for Measure* and *Love's Labour's Lost.* These plays are 'grounded on impossibilities, or at least, so meanly written, that the comedy neither caused your mirth, nor the serious part your concernment.' The novelist and critic Charlotte Lennox (*c.*1729–1804) regarded the statue scene as 'a low . . . contrivance' (Dobson and Wells: 524). It was not until the later years of the twentieth century that the drama began to really attract serious critical attention. This focuses upon its verbal ambiguities, use of ritual and seasonal movement from winter to summer, generic qualities relating to tragedy and comedy, depiction of jealousy and various kinds of sexuality, art and illusion, use of the pastoral, and ambiguous climax and conclusion. Deborah T. Curren-Aquino, in her 'Introduction' to her edition of *The New Cambridge Shakespeare: 'The Winter's Tale'* (2007), considers it to be 'a play that accepts imperfections and change . . . as part of life . . . Beginning with the contingency of "if" and ending with the discordance of "dissevered" [separated] echoing in the ear.' She adds that, 'Shakespeare's bittersweet tale of winter may be the miracle play for the twenty-first century' (61–62).

The Tempest

The Tempest is the first play to appear in the 1623 *First Folio*, although it probably is one of Shakespeare's last and regarded historically as embodying his theatrical farewell. The text contains elaborate stage directions, suggesting to some that Shakespeare added these in his Stratford retirement. Its first printed appearance in the *First Folio* as the first play has been taken to suggest that the text was received last at the printer's. This is speculation; what is known is that its first documented performance took place at the King's Court on 1 November 1611.

The play is influenced by contemporary sources, none of which were available prior to late 1610. The first is probably drawn upon for the tempest and shipwreck of the opening scene. William Strachey (fl. 1588–1620) travelled to Virginia on the *Sea-Adventure* in 1609. The ship went down off the Bermuda coast. His account of this circulated in the form of a prose letter but was not published until 1625. *A True Repertory of the Wrack and Redemption of Sir Thomas Gates* was circulated in manuscript form following its completion in Virginia in July 1610 and Gates' (d. 1622) arrival back in London in early September 1610. Another source relates to a journey to the New World. Sylvester Jordan (d. 1650) also travelled on the *Sea-Adventure*. His *A Discovery of the Bermudas, Otherwise Called the Isle of Divels* was published late in 1610 and the dedication is dated 13 October 1610. It reports that some on board the ship took to the bottle during the storm. To use Antonio's words in the first scene of *The Tempest*, 'We are merely cheated of our lives by drunkards' (56), and Caliban subsequently in the play refers to 'celestial liquor' (2. 2. 117).

In addition to the 1 November 1611 court performance, *The Tempest* was performed as part of the celebration in February 1613 for the marriage of Elizabeth Stuart. This may explain the goddess' masque in scene one of the fourth act. Dryden commented that the play had been earlier performed at the Blackfriars Theatre and theatrical tradition assigns Richard Burbage to the role of Prospero. Dryden's very popular *The Tempest, or The Enchanted Island* dates from 1667. Henry Purcell (1659–1695) in 1690 composed a score for Thomas Shadwell's 1674 operatic version, *The Enchanted Island*. This was performed regularly until well into the nineteenth century. Indeed, the play and versions of it, cinematic and other, remains popular today.

The Tempest seems to have attracted many creative artists and especially composers. Hector Berlioz (1803–1869) in 1830, Peter Tchaikovsky (1840–1893) in 1873 and Ralph Vaughan Williams (1872–1958) in 1951, all composed notable symphonic fantasies and song settings inspired by the drama. Poetic appropriation extends from Robert Browning's (1812–1889) dramatic monologue 'Caliban Upon Setebos; or, Natural Theology in the Island' (1859) to Ted Hughes' (1930–1998) poem 'Setebos' ([1998]), with its opening line 'Who could play Miranda?' The name of the major poetic collection of Hughes' first wife Sylvia Plath (b. 1932), who committed suicide in 1963, is *Ariel* (1965).

Perhaps the most well-known poetic response to the play is that of W. H. Auden (1907–1973), whose lengthy 'The Sea and the Mirror' (1944) has for its subtitle 'A commentary on Shakespeare's *The Tempest*'. In this, Auden encapsulates much of his critical perceptions of the play. Written during the Second World War, Auden's poem opens following the play's conclusion. As he prepares to leave the island, Prospero says to Ariel, 'in all, things have turned out better | Then I once expected or ever deserved.' Following his farewell to Ariel, the poem moves to the other participants: Alonso, Ferdinand and Miranda and the others accommodating to the 'darkness that we acknowledge ours'. Auden represents 'Caliban as Prospero's mirrored face-the magus's of art and secret self-[that] embodies libidinous forces that are normally repressed behind veneers of civility.'[16] Auden's essay on *The Tempest* in his collection *The Dyer's Hand* (1962) should not be ignored. In it, Auden posits the proposal that Ariel is Prospero's espionage agent!

Conclusion

The Tempest may be perceived as an echo chamber, a resume or revisiting of Shakespeare's motifs and themes. It is the story of loss and recovery (cf. *Pericles*, *The Winter's Tale* and *Cymbeline*). The play depicts the necessity for a father to let his daughter go and thus resonates with, for instance, *King Lear* and *Othello*. The treacherous betrayal of a legitimate ruler by a brother or a family member is also depicted, for instance, in *Richard II*, *Julius Caesar*, *Hamlet* and *Macbeth*, as is the murderous hatred of one brother for another in *Richard III*, *As You Like It*, *Hamlet*, and of a different gender, in *King Lear*. Prospero's exile from the court society and his voyage to the wilderness mirrors *Twelfth Night*, the retreat into a strange forest in *A Midsummer Night's Dream* and elements of *As You Like It*.

The Tempest contains more music, more songs, more dancing, more ballet and masques, in other words, more contemporary theatrical devices, than any other of Shakespeare's plays. The past contains tragic events; the present contains the enactment of reconciliation; and the future holds the promise of renewal. Indeed, in no other Shakespeare play is time more prominent, as if echoing the sense that time is running out for the dramatist, too. Prospero's magic depends upon precise timing. His first concern following the storm is with time. He tells his agent, Ariel, 'The time 'twixt six and now | Must by us both be spent most preciously' (1. 2. 240–241). The word 'now' occurs 79 times in the play, as if reinforcing the sense that the past is a prologue and the present is what matters.

Reconciliation for past wrongs is seemingly satisfactorily resolved through magical powers and transformation. Unique in Shakespeare's work, *The Tempest* unites the positive and the negative aspects of expulsion and exile. A creative artist conjuring up storms and tempests and apparently transforming the dead into the living, Prospero is dependant upon his book and his staff. Both crucial to his creative abilities, he 'abjure[s]', he 'break[s]' his 'staff,' further 'deeper than did ever plummet sound | I'll drown my book' (5. 1. 51, 54–55).

In a play dominated by allusions, spectacle and theatrical imagery, Prospero's farewell to his art and to his powers in the first scene of the fourth act has frequently been regarded as Shakespeare's own farewell to his theatre and premonition of his own death. The words

movingly echo the transitory nature of theatrical experience and of
life itself:

> And like the baseless fabric of this vision,
> The cloud-capp'd tow'rs, the gorgeous palaces,
> The solemn temples, the great globe itself,

Even the objects that are physically rooted and fixed, the 'globe' can
refer to the theatre or to the universe: 'Yea, all which it inherit, shall
dissolve,' the past, the present and even that in the future, are all
conveyed by the resonating pronoun 'it':

> And like this insubstantial pageant faded [the play, life itself]
> Leave not a rack behind. We are such stuff
> As dreams are made on; and our little life
> Is rounded with a sleep (4. 1. 151–158).

Ironically, placed in the perspective of such marvellous poetic
language with its reverberating assonance, consonants and repetitive
monosyllables, Caliban's comment to Miranda 'You taught me lan-
guage, and my profit on't | Is, I know how to curse' (1. 2. 363–364)
is juxtaposed with snatches of Caliban's lyric poetry. He dreams of
'a thousand twangling instruments' (3.2. 137). It is perceptions
of Caliban as an oppressed victim of colonial oppression represented
by Prospero that have dominated recent criticism of *The Tempest* and
ensured that its afterlife has undergone a renewed envigoration.[17]

Chapter Ten
Conclusion: Shakespeare's Life Enshrined. The First Folio

The appearance of the *First Folio* of *Mr. William Shakespeares Comedies, Histories & Tragedies* in 1623, seven years following his death, is a tremendous tribute to his life and work and an investment in the long-term staying power of Shakespeare's achievement. Anthony James West's *The Shakespeare First Folio: The History of the Book* (2001) notes that, at the end of the twentieth century, around 230 copies of the original 1,000 copies of probably the most important book in English literature are known to have survived. Only two are privately owned with the rest in institutional hands. The *First Folio* is the first collected edition of Shakespeare's work, although it excludes his poems. In short, it is his legacy.

The *First Folio* is primarily the work of two of Shakespeare's friends and fellow actors, to both of whom he left legacies, John Heminges and Henry Condell. It is thought that they teamed up with others to protect their rights and those of their recently deceased colleague when they learnt that a rival printer and publisher, Thomas Pavier (d. 1625), who had reprinted ten of Shakespeare's works individually in quarto form, was in 1619 planning a collection of the works. Following ten lines addressed 'To the Reader' and signed 'B.I.' [Ben Jonson], the *First Folio* has a prose epistle of explanation by John Heminges and Henry Condell concerning publication. This explanation is dedicated to William Herbert, 3rd Earl of Pembroke, to his brother Philip Herbert, the Earl of Montgomery (1584–1650), and to King James I. From such a dedication, it is clear that the two brothers acted as patrons for the King's Men and for Shakespeare. Heminges and Condell write that they have collected their colleague's work 'without ambition either of selfe-profit, or fame: onely to keep the memory of so worthy a Friend, & Fellow aliue, as was our *Shakespeare*'.

In the address that follows, 'To the Great Variety of Readers', they write, 'It has bene a thing, we confesse, worthie to have bene wished, that the Author himselfe had liud to haue set forth, and ouerseen his owne writings.' They continue, 'But since it hath bin ordin'd otherwise . . . we pray you do not envie his Friends, the office of their care, and paine, to haue collected & publish'd them.'

The colophon (note on the final page of the folio) indicates the cost of printing. The volume is 'Printed at the Charges of W. Jaggard, Ed. Blount, I. Smithweeke, and W. Aspley, 1623.' William Jaggard and his son, Isaac, were well-known London printers and in 1619 had printed nine quartos for Thomas Pavier. Edward Blount's name appears in the Stationers' Register in 1608 with *Pericles*, yet he never published it. John Smethwick (d. 1641) possessed rights to *Hamlet*, *Romeo and Juliet*, *Love's Labour's Lost* and *The Taming of the Shrew*. And William Aspley (d. 1640), another London printer and publisher, had rights on *Henry IV, Part II* and *Much Ado About Nothing*. Blount was not a printer, and the scholarship of Charlton Hinman (1911– 1977) has shown that the printing was carried out by the Jaggards. The printing of the 907 page folio started early in 1622 and took almost two years to finish, with up to nine compositors working on the project. Work by Trevor Howard-Hill (b. 1933) has shown that Ralph Crane (fl. 1555–1632), played an important role in the transcription of the original play scripts into printer's copy.[18]

It was Heminges and Condell who subdivided the plays into 'Comedies', 'Histories' and 'Tragedies'. The exception is *Troilus and Cressida*. This is omitted from the *First Folio* table of contents, although the text is included under 'Tragedies'. In addition, there are commendatory verses: two by Ben Jonson, and one each by Hugh Holland, Leonard Digges, and probably James Mabbe. Hugh Holland (d. 1623) from Trinity College, Cambridge, contributes a sonnet, 'Upon the Lines and Life of the Famous Scenicke Poet Master William Shakespeare.' He establishes that Shakespeare existed and has died: 'his dayes are done, that made the dainty Playes | Which made the Globe of heau'n and earth to ring.' He pays tribute to the poetry, to his '*Tragedies*', to his '*Fame*', and concludes with the rhyming couplet, 'For though his line of life went soone about, | The life yet of his lines shall neuer out.'

Leonard Digges (1588–1635), an Oxford-educated Londoner, had some connection with Shakespeare. In his will, Shakespeare leaves money to Thomas Russell (1570–1634), a local Stratford landowner who studied at Queen's College, Oxford and in 1603 married Digges' mother, Anne. The 1623 folio contains the first of Digges' poetic tributes to Shakespeare. The second of 68 lines is found in the 1640 volume of Shakespeare's *Poems,* published by John Benson (d. 1667). The initial folio tribute consists of 22 lines and contains the first extant allusion to a monument to Shakespeare at the Stratford Holy Trinity Church. Digges writes, when 'Time dissolves thy *Stratford* Moniment'. In addition to references to *Romeo and Juliet* and the Roman plays, the Shakespeare who wrote the plays is the William Shakespeare of Stratford. There is no room for pretenders. Digges concludes, 'Be sure, our *Shake-speare*, thou canst neuer dye, | But crown'd with Lawrell, liue eternally.'

The poems conclude with an eight-line elegy 'To the Memorie of M. W. Shake-Speare', written by 'I.M.' These lines have been attributed to James Mabbe (1572–1642), a Fellow of Magdalen College, Oxford. In the lines, Shakespeare departs from the 'World's-Stage to the Graues-Tyring-roome', however, 'Wee thought thee dead, but this thy printed worth'.

By far the most interesting, and in some instances enigmatic portion of the introductory material to the enshrinement in print of Shakespeare's memory, is the 88-line 'To The Memory of My Beloued, the Avthor Mr. William Shakespeare: And What he has left vs' by Ben Jonson. This is the second poetic tribute in the Folio by Jonson, the most celebrated dramatist of the age and in a very real sense Shakespeare's rival. The first is found on the preliminary page and consists of ten lines addressed 'To the Reader', focusing on the image of Shakespeare found on the facing title page. This contains the so-called 'Droeshout' portrait or engraving, the work of Martin Droeshout the elder (*c.*1560–1642), a Flemish engraver and refugee who settled in England. It appears to be a retrospective commission and Jonson's lines testify to its being Shakespeare. Jonson tells the reader: 'This Figure, that thou here seest put, | It was for gentle Shakespeare cut.' Jonson continues:

> O, could he but haue drawne his wit
> As well in brasse, as he hath hit
> His face: the Print would then surpasse
> All, that vvas euer vvrit in brasse.
> But, since he cannot, Reader, looke
> Not on his Picture, but his Booke.

According to Peter Holland in his *Oxford Dictionary of National Biography* account of Shakespeare, 'This image of Shakespeare with its massive dome of a forehead . . . concealing, it seems to imply, a brain of disproportionate size, has become one of the most potent icons of Western culture.' Holland continues, 'the very essence of the originating author making his presence visible in connection with his works.'

Jonson's other lines are complex. They are a tribute to a rival but contain negatives as well. John Dryden regarded Jonson's 'To the Memory of my Beloued . . .' as 'an insolent, sparing, and invidious panegyric.' Perhaps Dryden had in mind Jonson's observations in *Timber, or Discoveries*: 'hee flow'd with that facility, that sometime it was necessary he should be stop'd . . . His wit was his owne power; would the rule of it had been so too' (Lipking: 140–141). Earlier in *Timber*, Jonson observed: 'I loved the man, and do honour his memory – on this side idolatry – as much as any. He was, indeed, and of an open and free nature; had an excellent fantasy [imagination], brave notions [admirable ideas], and gentle expressions [a dignified way of expressing them].'

The initial 16 lines of Jonson's eulogy are concerned with the correct way of praising Shakespeare, and the real eulogy starts at line 17: 'I, therefore will begin. Soule of the Age! | The applause! delight! the wonder of our Stage!' The eulogy reveals very little about Shakespeare as a human being or as a poet, except that he 'hadst small *Latine* and less Greeke' (31). After surveying the record of tragic and comic forms and the criteria for a first-class poet, the 'Sweet Swan of *Auon*' (71) becomes part of the firmament.

Jonson praises Shakespeare's art and craftsmanship: 'of *Shakespeare's* minde, and manners brightly shines | In his well tourned, and true-filed lines.' Shakespeare's work out 'shine[s]' (67–68) his contemporaries such as John Lily (1553/4–1606), 'or sporting *Kid*, or *Marlowes* mighty line' (30). Shakespeare has no equals: 'He was not of an age, but for all time!' He is beyond an age, indeed, is ageless. His achievements reflect upon his country, such as when Jonson writes, 'my *Britaine*! Thou hast one to showe | To whom all Scenes of *Europe* homage owe' (41–42). Even he has to praise Shakespeare: 'Shine forth, thou Starre of *Poets*, and with rage, | Or influence, chide or cheere the drooping Stage' (77–78). It is no accident that the immortalization of Shakespeare's *First Folio* should conclude with 'The Names of the Principall Actors in All These Playes', beginning with William Shakespeare himself and followed by Richard Burbage and John Heminges.[19]

In 1916, to commemorate the three hundredth anniversary of Shakespeare's death, the Oxford University Press issued a sumptuous volume of tributes. Called *1916 A Book of Homage to Shakespeare,* the volume was edited by the eminent Medieval and Renaissance scholar Sir Israel Gollancz (1864–1930), a Fellow of the British Academy and Honorary Secretary of the Shakespeare Tercentenary Committee. The volume gives prominent place to 'To Shakespeare After 300 Years', a six-stanza verse of six lines each dated 'February 14, 1916', in other words, St. Valentine's Day, and written in the midst of World War I by the pre-eminent poet of the day Thomas Hardy (1840–1928). 'Through human orbits thy discourse to-day . . . throbs on', writes Hardy. Hardy recognizes that '"I" faith, few knew him . . . save by word' and notes, in typical Hardy fashion, that 'Death comes to all' ([1]–2). No doubt in 2016, the Hardy of the time will compose similar sentiments to Shakespeare, hopefully not in the midst of another war. To use Ben Jonson's words, Shakespeare 'was not of an age, but for all time!' (43).

Notes

1. For an account of these other candidates, see Michael Dobson and Stanley Wells, ed. *The Oxford Companion to Shakespeare*: 106 and Jonathan Bate's *The Genius of Shakespeare* (1997): 57, and his *Soul of the Age: The Life, Mind and World of Shakespeare* (2008): 185–186, 219–221.
2. Noteworthy readings of the poem range from A. Alvarez 'Shakespeare's "The Phoenix and The Turtle"' in *Interpretations: Essays on Twelve English Poems*, ed. John Wain (1955), Nicholas Birns, '*The Phoenix and Turtle*' in *The Greenwood Companion to Shakespeare*, ed. J. Rosenblum; (2005): IV, 1309–1322, William Empson, '*The Phoenix and the Turtle*' in *Essays in Criticism*, 15 (1966): 147–153 and G. Wilson Knight, *The Mutual Flame: On Shakespeare's Sonnets, and The Phoenix and the Turtle* (1955). Recent interpretations are put forward in Katherine Duncan-Jones, and H. R. Woudhuysen, eds, *The Poems – Arden Shakespeare. Third Series*, ed. (2007) – see 99–123, 420, 428.
3. For discussion on the relations between Spenser and Shakespeare, see essays in J. B. Lethbridge, ed. *Shakespeare and Spenser: Attractive Opposites*, (2008).
4. For a detailed description of a soliloquy and its Shakespearean usage, see James E. Hirsh, *Shakespeare and the History of Soliloquies*, (2003).
5. For a discussion of Elizabethan and Jacobean religious differences in attitudes towards ghosts see Stephen Greenblatt in 'The Touch of the Real', in Sherry B. Ortner, ed. *The Fate of Culture: Geertz and Beyond*: 24–28 and Stephen Greenblatt, *Hamlet in Purgatory* (2001): 47–101.
6. See *The Warwick Shakespeare Deed*, London, Sotheby's, (1997): [5–9].
7. For a new historicist reading of the play, see Jonathan Dollimore 'Transgression and Surveillance in *Measure for Measure*' in *Political Shakespeare*, ed. J. Dollimore and A. Seinfield: 72–87. For feminist readings see Carolyn Asp, 'Subjectivity, Desire and Female Friendship in *All's Well That Ends Well*', *Literature and Psychology*, 32 (1986):

48–61 and Luigi D. Gangi, 'Pleasure and Danger: Measuring Female Sexuality in *Measure for Measure*', *Journal of English Literary History*, 60 (1993): 589–609. See also the excellent account of the problems of interpreting the play by Barbara Everett in her 'A Dreame of Passion', *London Review of Books*, 2 January 2003: 23–26.

8. See for instance the essays in Simon Barker's *New Casebooks: Shakespeare's Problem Plays. All's Well That Ends Well, Measure for Measure, Troilus and Cressida* (2005) and Katharine Eisaman Maus in *The Norton Shakespeare Based on the Oxford Edition*. Second edition.: 2193–2199.

9. For an account of these see Anthony B. Dawson's 'New Cambridge Edition' of the play (2003): 46–66 and see also 67–70 'A Note on the Text'.

10. See Peter Blayney, 'The Booke of *Sir Thomas More* Re-Examined', *Studies in Philology* 69 (1972), 167–191; A. C. Partridge, 'The Manuscript Play *Sir Thomas More*: List of Contractions in Dramatic Use by 1600', in his *Orthography in Shakespeare and Elizabethan Drama: A Study of Colloquial Contractions, Elision, Prosody and Punctuation* (1964): 43–66.

11. See MacDonald P. Jackson, *Defining Shakespeare: Pericles as Test Case* (2003).

12. See J. L. Halio's edition, *King Henry VIII, or All Is True*. Oxford: Oxford University Press (1999).

13. Gordon McMullen, 'Fletcher, John,' *ODNB*, and citing Lois Potter, ed. *The Two Noble Kinsmen*, Arden Edition (1997): 1. For a thorough account of the attribution issue, see Vickers, *Shakespeare, Co-Author*: 402–432.

14. See E. A. J. Honigmann and S. Brock, eds, *Playhouse Wills 1558-1642: An Edition of Wills by Shakespeare and His Contemporaries in the London Theatre* (1993): 113, 157.

15. See for instance the contributions to Alison Thorne, ed., *New Casebooks: Shakespeare's Romances*, edited, (2000).

16. Virginia Mason Vaughan and Auden T. Vaughan III, eds, *The Arden Shakespeare: The Tempest*. (1999): 111.

17. See for instance the essays in Alison Thorne's *New Casebooks: Shakespeare's Romances*.

18. See Charlton B. Hinman, *The Printing and Proofreading of the First Folio of Shakespeare* 2 vols. (1963) and Trevor Howard-Hill,

'Shakespeare's Earliest Editor, Ralph Crane', *Shakespeare Survey* 44 (1992): 113–129 and *Ralph Crane and Some Shakespeare's First Folio Comedies* (1972). For a modernized spelling text of the First Folio, see the Jonathan Bate and Eric Rasmussen, eds, *RSC Shakespeare*, ed. (2007). For the subsequent Folios, see Dobson and Wells, *The Oxford Companion to Shakespeare*: 147.
19. For a detailed discussion of Jonson's eulogy see Lawrence Lipking, *The Life of the Poet: Beginning and Ending Poetic Careers* (1981): 138–145.

Bibliography

The following collected editions of Shakespeare have been used.

Bate, Jonathan and Eric Rasmussen, eds *The RSC Shakespeare*. Houndmills, Basingstoke: Macmillan Palgrave, 2007.

Evans, G. Blakemore and J. J. M. Tobin, general eds *The Riverside Shakespeare*, Second edition. Boston, New York: Houghton Mifflin, 1997.

Greenblatt, Stephen, Walter Cohen, Jean E. Howard and Katharine Eisaman Maus, eds *The Norton Shakespeare Based on the Oxford Edition*. Second edition. New York, London: W.W. Norton & Co., 2008.

Hinman, Charlton, ed. *The First Folio of Shakespeare*. New York: W.W. Norton, 1996.

Individual Editions

Hamlet, ed. Harold Jenkins. Arden Edition. London: Methuen, 1982.

Hamlet, ed. Ann Thompson and Neil Taylor. Arden Edition. London: Thomson Learning, 2006

Henry V. ed. T. W. Craik. Arden Edition. London: Routledge, 1995.

King Henry VIII, or All Is True. ed. J. L. Halio. Oxford: Oxford University Press, 1999.

The Poems – Arden Shakespeare. Third Series. ed. Katherine Duncan-Jones and H. R. Woudhuysen. London: Thomson Learning, 2007.

The Tempest. ed. Virginia Mason Vaughan and Auden T. Vaughan, III. Arden Edition. London: Thomas Nelson, 1999.

Timon of Athens. ed. Anthony B. Dawson and Gretchen E. Minton. Arden Edition. London: Cengage Learning, 2008.

Troilus and Cressida. ed. Anthony B. Dawson. New Cambridge Edition. Cambridge University Press, 2003.

Twelfth Night. ed. J. M. Lothian and T. W. Craik. Arden Edition. London: Thomson Learning, 2001.

Two Noble Kinsmen. ed. Lois Potter. Arden Edition. London: Nelson, 1997.

The Winter's Tale. ed. Deborah T. Curren-Aquino. New Cambridge Edition. Cambridge University Press, 2007.

Writing about Shakespeare and General Works

Abrams, M. H. *A Glossary of Literary Terms*. Eighth Edition. Boston, MA: Thomson Higher Education, 2005.

Adelman, Janet. *Suffocating Mothers: Fantasies of Maternal Origin in Shakespeare's Plays, 'Hamlet' to 'The Tempest'*. London: Routledge, 1991.

Alvarez, A. 'The Phoenix and the Turtle', in *Interpretations: Essays on Twelve English Poems*. ed. John Wain. London: Routledge (1955): 1–16.

Asp, Carolyn. 'Subjectivity, Desire and Female Friendship in *All's Well That Ends Well*', *Literature and Psychology*, 32 (1986): 48–61.

Asquith, Clare. *Shadowplay: The Hidden Beliefs and Coded Politics of William Shakespeare*. New York: Public Affairs, 2005.

Baker, William and Brian Vickers, ed. *Shakespeare: The Critical Tradition. The Merchant of Venice*. London and New York: Thoemmes, 2005.

Barbour, Reid. 'Peele, George', *Oxford Dictionary of National Biography* (www.oxforddnb.com).

Barker, Simon, ed. *New Casebooks: Shakespeare's Problem Plays. All's Well That Ends Well, Measure for Measure, Troilus and Cressida*. Houndmills, Basingstoke, Hants: Palgrave Macmillan, 2005.

Barton, Anne. 'Leontes and the Spider: Language and Speaker in Shakespeare's Last Plays', in *Essays, Mainly Shakespearian*. Cambridge: Cambridge University Press (1994): 161–181.

Bate, Jonathan. *The Genius of Shakespeare*. London: Picador, 1997.

—*Soul of the Age: The Life, Mind and World of Shakespeare*. London: Viking/Penguin, 2008.

—'Dampit and Moll', *TLS* (April 25, 2008): 3–5, 7 (review of Taylor and Lavagnino).

Battenhouse, Roy W. '*Measure for Measure* and the Doctrine of Atonement', *PMLA*, 6 (1946): 1029–1059.

Birns, Nicholas. 'The Phoenix and the Turtle', in *The Greenwood Companion to Shakespeare*, ed. J. Rosenblum, 4 vols., Westport, CT: Greenwood, 2005: IV: 1309–1322.

Blayney, Peter. 'The Booke of Sir Thomas More Re-Examined', *Studies in Philology*, 69 (1972): 167–191.

Boas, Frederick Samuel. *Shakespeare and His Predecessors*. London: John Murray, 1896.

Boyd, Brian, ed. *Words that Count: Essays in Early Modern Authorship in Honor of MacDonald P. Jackson*. Cranbury, NJ: Associated University Presses, 2004.

Bradley, Andrew. *Shakespearean Tragedy*. London: Macmillan, 2004.

Cerasano, S. P. 'Philip Henslowe and the Elizabethan Court', *Shakespeare Survey*, 60 (2007): 49–57.

Chambers, E. K. *William Shakespeare: A Study of Facts and Problems*. 2 vols. Oxford: Clarendon Press, 1930.

Croft, P. J. *Autograph Poetry and the English Language: Facsimiles of Original Manuscripts from the Fourteenth to the Twentieth Century*. 2 vols., London: Cassell, 1973.

Dobson, Michael and Stanley Wells, eds *The Oxford Companion to Shakespeare*. Oxford: Oxford University Press, 2001.

Dollimore, Jonathan. 'Transgression and Surveillance in *Measure for Measure*', in *Political Shakespeare: New Essays in Cultural Materialism*, ed. Jonathon Dollimore and Alan Sinfield. Ithaca: Cornell University Press, 1985: 72–87.

Dillon, Janette. 'From Revels to Revelation: Shakespeare and the Mask', *Shakespeare Survey*, 60 (2007): 58–71.

Duncan-Jones, Katherine. 'Review of Nicoll', *TLS* (December 14, 2007): 25.

Empson, William. 'The Phoenix and the Turtle', *Essays in Criticism*, 15, 1966: 147–153.

Everett, Barbara. 'A Dreame of Passion', *London Review of Books* (January 2, 2003): 23–26.

Foakes, R. A., ed. *Henslowe's Diary*. Second Edition. Cambridge: Cambridge University Press, 2002.

Gangi, Luigi, D. 'Pleasure and Danger: Measuring Female Sexuality in *Measure for Measure*', *The Journal of English Literary History*, 60 (1993): 586–609.

Gollancz, Sir Israel, ed. *1916 A Book of Homage to Shakespeare*. London: Oxford University Press, 1916.

Greenblatt, Stephen. *Hamlet in Purgatory*. Princeton, NJ: Princeton University Press, 2001.

—'The Touch of the Real', in Sherry B. Ortner, ed. *The Fate of Culture: Geertz and Beyond*. Berkeley and Los Angeles, CA: University of California Press, 1999: 14–29.

—*Will in the World: How Shakespeare Became Shakespeare*. London and New York: Norton, 2004.

—Walter Cohen, Jean E. Howard, and Katharine Eisaman Maus, ed. *The Norton Shakespeare Based on the Oxford Edition*. Second Edition. New York, London: W. W. Norton & Co., 2008.

Greer, Germaine. *Shakespeare's Wife*. New York: Harper Collins, 2007.

Gurr, Andrew. 'The Glory of the Globe', *TLS* (October 18, 1991): 5–6.

Hinman, Charlton B. *The Printing and Proofreading of the First Folio of Shakespeare*. 2 vols., Oxford: Oxford University Press, 1963.

Hirsh, James E. *Shakespeare and the History of Soliloquies*. Cranbury, NJ: Associated University Presses, 2003.

Holland, Peter. 'Shakespeare, William'. *Oxford Dictionary of National Biography* (www.oxforddnb.com).

Honan, Park. *Shakespeare: A Life*. Oxford: Oxford University Press, Honan, Park . . . 1998.

Honigmann, E. A. J. *Shakespeare: The 'Lost Years'*. Second Edition. Manchester and New York: Manchester University Press, 1998.

—Honigmann, E. A. J. and S. Brock, eds *Playhouse Wills 1558-1642: An Edition of Wills by Shakespeare and His Contemporaries in the London Theatre*. Manchester: Manchester University Press, 1993.

Howard-Hill, Trevor H. *Ralph Crane and Some Shakespeare First Folio Comedies*. Charlottesville, VA: Bibliographical Society of the University of Virginia, 1972.

—ed. *Shakespeare and 'Sir Thomas More': Essays on the Play and Its Shakespearean Interest*. Cambridge: Cambridge University Press, 1999.

—'Shakespeare's Earliest Editor, Ralph Crane', *Shakespeare Survey*, 44 (1992): 113–129.

Jackson, MacDonald, P. 'The Date and Authorship of Hand D's Contribution to *Sir Thomas More*: Evidence From "Literature on Line"', *Shakespeare Survey*, 59 (2006): 69–78.

—'Hand D of *Sir Thomas More*', *Notes and Queries*, 226 (1981): 146.

—*Defining Shakespeare: Pericles as Test Case*. Oxford: Oxford University Press, 2003.

Jakobson, Roman and Lawrence G. Jones. *Shakespeare's Verbal Art in Th' Expence of Spirit*. The Hague, Paris: Mouton, 1970.

Kermode, Frank. *Shakespeare's Language*. London: Allen Lane, The Penguin Press, 2000.

Knight, G. Wilson. *The Crown of Life: Essays in Interpretation of Shakespeare's Final Plays*. Oxford: Oxford University Press, 1947.

— *The Mutual Flame: On Shakespeare's Sonnets and the Phoenix and the Turtle*. London: Methuen, 1955.

— *The Wheel of Fire: Essays in Interpretation of Shakespeare's Sombre Tragedies*. London: Oxford University Press, 1930.

Lanier, Emilia. *The Poems of Shakespeare's Dark Lady*. *Salve Deux Rex Judaeorum*. Introduction by A. L. Rowse. London: Jonathan Cape, 1978.

Law, R. A. 'The Double Authorship of *Henry VIII*', *Studies in Philology*, 56 (1959): 471–486.

Lawrence, W. W. *Shakespeare's Problem Comedies: Studies in Form and Meaning*. New York: Macmillan, 1931.

Leavis, F. R. '*Antony and Cleopatra* and *All For Love*. A Critical Exercise', *Scrutiny*, 5, (September 1936): 158–169.

Lethbridge, J. B. (ed.) *Shakespeare and Spenser: Attractive Opposites*. Manchester: Manchester University Press, 2008.

Lipking, Lawrence. *The Life of the Poet: Beginning and Ending Poetic Careers*. Chicago: University of Chicago Press, 1981.

Matthew, H. G. C., Brian Harrison and Lawrence Goldman, eds *Oxford Dictionary of National Biography in Association with the British Academy from the Earliest Times to the Year 2000* [and updates]. Oxford: Oxford University Press and British Academy, 2004. Online www.oxforddnb.com.

McDonald, Russ. *The Bedford Companion to Shakespeare: An Introduction with Documents*. Second Edition. Boston, MA, New York: Bedford/St. Martin's, 2001.

— *Shakespeare's Later Style*. Cambridge: Cambridge University Press, 2006.

Melchiori, Giorgio. 'Hand D in *Sir Thomas More*: An Essay in Misinterpretation', *Shakespeare Survey*, 38 (1985): 101–114.

Middleton, Thomas. *The Collected Works*, ed. Gary Taylor and John Lavagnino. Oxford: Oxford University Press, 2007.

Moore Smith, G. C. *Gabriel Harvey's Marginalia*. Stratford-upon-Avon: Shakespeare Head Press, 1913.

Nicoll, Charles. *The Lodger: Shakespeare on Silver Street*. London: Allen Lane, 2007. [American edition entitled *The Lodger Shakespeare: His Life on Silver Street*. New York: Viking, 2008].

Norman, Marc and Tom Stoppard. *Shakespeare in Love: A Screenplay*. New York: Hyperion Miramax, 1998.

Nuttall, A. D. *Shakespeare the Thinker*. New Haven and London: Yale University Press, 2007.

Nye, Robert. *Mrs. Shakespeare: The Complete Works*. Harmondsworth: Penguin Books, 1993.

Parr, Anthony. 'Wilkins, George'. Oxford Dictionary of National Biography (www.oxforddnb.com)

Partridge, A. C. *Orthography in Shakespeare and Elizabethan Drama: A Study of Colloquial Contractions, Elision Prosody and Punctuation*. London: Arnold, 1964.

Rowse, A. L. *Discovering Shakespeare*. London: Weidenfeld and Nicolson Limited, 1989.

—*Shakespeare the Man*. London: Macmillan, 1973.

Schoenbaum, Samuel. *Shakespeare's Lives*. New Edition. Oxford: Clarendon Press, 1991.

Shaheen, Naseeb. *Biblical References in Shakespeare's Plays*. Cranbury, NJ: Associated University Presses, 1999.

Taylor, Gary. 'Middleton, Thomas', *Oxford Dictionary of National Biography* (www.oxforddnb.com).

Taylor, Gary and John Lavagnino. *Thomas Middleton and Early Modern Textual Culture: A Companion to the Collected Works*. Oxford: Oxford University Press, 2007.

Thorne, Alison, ed. *New Casebooks: Shakespeare's Romances*. Houndmills, Basingstoke, Hants: Palgrave Macmillan, 2000.

Vickers, Brian. 'Kyd's Authorship of about two-thirds of *1 Henry VI* (*Letters*, TLS, May 16, 2008): 6.

—*Shakespeare, Co-Author: A Historical Study of Five Collaborative Plays*. Oxford: Oxford University Press, 2002.

The Warwick Shakespeare Deed. London: Sotheby's, 11 December 1997. Supplement [to] English Literature and History. Sotheby's London, Thursday 11 December 1997 (Auction Catalogue).

Weis, René. *Shakespeare Unbound: Decoding a Hidden Life*. New York: Henry Holt, 2007.

Wells, Stanley. *Shakespeare and Co.* New York: Pantheon Books, 2006.

West, Anthony James. *The Shakespeare First Folio: The History of the Book*. 2 vols., Oxford: Oxford University Press, 2001, 2003.

Williams, William Proctor and Craig S. Abbott. *An Introduction to Bibliographical and Textual Studies*, Third Edition. New York: MLA, 1999.

Wilson, John Dover. *The Essential Shakespeare: A Biographical Adventure*. New York: Macmillan, 1932.

—*The Manuscript of Shakespeare's Hamlet and the Problems of Its Transmission*. New York: Macmillan, Cambridge: Cambridge University Press, 1934.

—*What Happens in Hamlet*. New York: Macmillan, Cambridge: Cambridge University Press, 1935.

Index